Crossing the Line

Sales Strategies for Life & Health in the P&C Agency

Robert S. Littell, CLU, ChFC, FLMI
& Larry McSpadden, CPCU, ARM

NATIONAL UNDERWRITER®
The Last Word For Over 100 Years

The National Underwriter Company
505 Gest Street
Cincinnati, Ohio 45203

First edition, 1997
second printing, 1998

International Standard Book Number: 0-87218-361-0

Printed in the United States of America

Dedication

Robert S. Littell:

For my wife, Carolyn, who just rolled her eyes when I told her I was co-authoring a book on top of juggling all the other "balls in the air," but who supported and goaded me through it all, as well as Lisa, my assistant, who interpreted my scribblings

Larry D. McSpadden:

For Thomas A. McSpadden, CPCU, CLU, ARM: honest, loving and insightful as a family and business leader

Table of Contents

Preface

The motivation for this book arose out of several conversations the authors had over the past three years about developing Life and Health ("L&H") sales opportunities in Property/Casualty ("P&C") agencies. Many of the ideas here arose from our own experience (50 years combined experience, as of this writing) working in the P&C and Life insurance industry. We first met at a conference in Chicago in 1994 whose theme was the future of alternative distribution methods in the insurance business. Bob led a "breakout session" on the role technology would play in the future of both L&H and P&C carriers, Larry attended the session. Afterward, they began talking about technology and insurance distribution, and have been talking ever since. The basic outline of this book arose from these conversations, but many of the particular insights and suggestions presented here were either confirmed by or originated from our colleagues and friends throughout the industry.

Acknowledgements

Robert S. Littell:

"Thanks to my many P&C friends who either directly or indirectly taught me what works and, more importantly, what doesn't work in getting P&C producers to write more life business and/or to refer clients to in-house life specialists or outside experts.

These include: Bill Parr, J. Smith Lanier, Jeff McCart, The McCart Agency; John Snellings, Snellings-Walters Insurance; Jack Hungelmann, Jack Hungelmann Insurance and Tom Yearian. J. Smith Lanier who produce two great home-grown newsletters; Charlie Adams, The Adams Group; Allen Jackson, Skelton-Morris Agency; and Mike Steiner, Michael Steiner & Associates. Special thanks to Chuck Wright at State Farm who shared some of their vision for the future and what it will take to get there."

Larry McSpadden:

"I would like to thank, first of all, my wife Jane, for her encouragement, support and understanding. Thanks also to all of my fellow employees at the Beauchamp & McSpadden and Morrison Galliher Agencies — especially Evan Beauchamp and Brent Webster for the great brainstorming sessions — we're getting there! Agency members of ARM of Indiana and of ARM International have provided a lot of ideas and direction in our many enjoyable meetings and discussions — with special thanks to Jim Talkington from the Salem Insurance Agency in Goshen, Indiana, and John Dils with the RMD Agency in Richmond, Indiana.

Consultants and speakers I've heard over the years about how to sell insurance have been marvelously consistent — the basics are the same, if the speaker knows the business, and these folks do; so, thanks to these people for repeating the same selling messages to me often enough that they finally "took hold": Dick Womack, Joan Sansing, Jack Fries, Mona Carpenter, and Larry Neilson. Finally, thanks to Rand Ruggeberg, our editor at the National Underwriter, who has been patiently and gently encouraging our efforts on this book. The insurance retailing business is vast and complicated, and we all owe so much to our predecessors and to each other — let's keep it going."

Introduction

Insurance retailers in North America face a great challenge. Our survival is threatened as societal, economic and technological forces question the traditional retailer's utility. The marketplace — the very arena in which we work for our livelihood — seeks to eliminate us. By automating or trivializing much of what we do, the insurance industry will accelerate its search for ways to do without — without the expense and trouble of dealing with us. The challenge is to survive, and — in these storms of rapid change — to maintain a steady and successful course into the future.

In this book, we will suggest and elaborate on several strategies for survival and success. We will introduce the need for, and develop discussions about:

- How to develop a robust sales culture
- How to implement successful marketing plans
- How to integrate significant life and related insurance sales into a P&C culture
- How to increase revenues per client and revenues per sales call
- How to use the marketing of non-insurance services to thwart insurance competitors
- How to take advantage of today's (and some of tomorrow's) technologies
- How to increase bottom-line returns from the limited resources at your command.

This book's fundamental premise is that the insurance marketplace has changed profoundly in recent years, and the context of this altered market suggests rich opportunities for those ready to take advantage of them (and dire consequences for those who choose to ignore them). While appearing chaotic, we believe that these changes arise from a few coherent and predictable sources. We hope to cut beneath the confusing surface and then identify and explain these deeper currents — pointing out their direction and suggesting how to realign your business activities with them.

While many challenges and pressures are squeezing today's agent and broker, the typical P&C organization stands in a position of considerable power — well-poised to leap into a prosperous and exciting future. Many of these retailers are not aware of this powerful opportunity. Because we believe in the inherent value of the insurance retailing function, it is our goal to encourage, assist and enhance the retailer's position, and leverage this power to promising new horizons.

This overlooked potential is an "off-balance sheet" asset, one that has not been adequately valued or appreciated by our predecessors. The unique strategic position of the insurance retailer arises out of two very obvious facts — we can sell intangibles and services, and we have established relationships with consumers. Banks are not historically used to marketing to their customers, preferring to react to their inquiries — direct sales is not their core business. Reinsurance companies and capital markets don't have direct relationships with the buying public. Insurance companies (with some exceptions) are not positioned to sell directly to consumers as effectively as we are..at least not until the "post-Boomer" generation arrives.

Consumers who need sophisticated financial products and services (typically) cannot get reliable product information, or efficient access to the marketplace, although the Internet is rapidly changing that. Insurance companies need current, dynamic underwriting information about their insureds; businesses and families need competent guidance in the areas of insurance products and the complex marketplace. So for the time being at least, we are still needed for most insurance transactions to be conducted.

Even in a rapidly-changing world, capital markets will continue to want the access to consumers that insurance retailers can provide. Financial markets are developing new products at an unprecedented, and accelerating pace — but will gain nothing without getting them sold in the market. Other service industries are looking for new ways to approach prospective customers, and see real economies beckoning if they don't have to develop, train and deploy their own sales force. More and more, many of these sources will be saying, "Maybe we can get insurance agents to sell these new products. They can sell anything, and they already know the very customers we want to reach!"

As insurance retailers, our "core competency" is (or should be) selling, and our principal asset (what transfers when an agency or brokerage is bought or sold) is our customer list or expiration list, i.e., our business relationships: our knowledge of, and history of interaction with, the prospect and customer. This book should make you better at the sales process itself, while expanding your horizons into new products and services that you should be selling. We hope to make clear, then, how such expanded selling activities will enhance and solidify your customer relationships, and how this in turn will lead to more revenue and more inherent value in your business.

Each section of this book will be directed toward "stepping up" the revenue cycles for any insurance retailer. We will discuss, in some detail, how to transfer these new sales habits into the lucrative life insurance field. It is hoped that the detailed template for life sales will be used as a model for further expansion into many other, related marketing areas, including insurance alternatives, group workplace marketing, employee benefits plans, loss control and similar services, business consulting, human resources outsourcing, and employee leasing sales.

Who Might Profit From Reading This Book

Challenges and opportunities stretch across the entire insurance industry, so readers working in most sub-sectors of the business will benefit from this material. Some of the principles and strategies to be discussed apply universally, and will help the single small-town direct writing agent, the producer for a mid-size independent agency, the sales manager at a regional broker, as well as the coordinating staff among the international mega-brokers. Each of these reader groups will find tips and tactics directed primarily at them (while learning what your different-sized competition groups might be planning or contemplating).

Insurance retailers manage a "triangular" business relationship, selling products and services that arise from the financial services industry, to their individual clients and customers. The retailer, company, and client are interdependently-connected in this business relationship. Accordingly, marketing managers and field marketers from P&C insurance companies would find much here of interest; after all, it pays to keep up with your sales force, appreciate their needs, and anticipate their strategic changes. Similarly, consumers of P&C insurance (particularly business consumers and in-house risk managers) could use this book to generate challenges for their current agent or broker: are they keeping up with the times... are they offering all in the way of innovation, valuable services, and business assistance that they might?

One of the primary themes developed throughout the book will show readers how to generate and expand life and health ("L&H") insurance sales in any P&C organizations. Whether you now have a "life department" or contemplate starting one, you will find many valuable nuggets of information here. Almost every P&C organization, from the retail "captive agents" to the international broker, to the direct mail and Internet vendor, is attempting to generate life and health insurance revenues, either internally or in concert with a corresponding company. Ironically, though, we have yet to hear of many, if any, that are taking *full* advantage of this potential revenue source. Until now, no one has quite figured out the ideal strategy or best approach to this problem. Top management in any P&C operation will want to know and apply at least some of the ideas found here on this topic.

L&H producers working in or with a P&C shop will get a lot of support and inspiration here (as will those who would like to join, or joint venture with, a friendly P&C organization). You, better than most, directly experience the missed opportunities, squandered resources, and bungled communications that typify most L&H sales efforts in P&C shops. You will learn here more about the underlying cultural differences between the two industry segments, and how to build bridges between them. You'll find tips for amplifying your "minority voice," and for developing profitable alliances with key people in the firm. After reading it, you'll probably want to bring this book to the attention of the President, Sales Manager, "Personal Lines" manager, and key P&C producers in your organization.

Marketing, agency development, and field staff for L&H companies will want to read and share this book — the implementation of the ideas presented here along your distribution channels will lead to increased production, market share, and persistency.

Certainly, Sales Managers in any insurance organization will want this book as a reference and for inspiration. You will find a re-framing of the sales management picture here that starts with the "basics," points out the direction toward a true "sales culture," and continues with multiple ideas for expanding into new sales opportunities. The Sales Manager's managers (i.e., Directors, Presidents and Principals of agencies and brokerage houses) will want to at least skim over this material as well, to get ideas for strategies and motivation tactics that will improve the financial performance of your business.

Ambitious, energetic P&C producers will quickly get the gist of this book — how to maximize success while limited to a finite number of hours available for sales. You'll be encouraged to "keep your head up" in scouting for new products and services, new ways to assist your customers and prospects with their business problems. We hope that folks on the P&C side will also gain some "sensitivity training" through their reading, and grow to better appreciate the particular needs and talents of their L&H compatriots..and vice versa.

As mentioned earlier, a secondary theme running through the book will be the expansion of selling opportunities for insurance retailers into product and service fields beyond those typically vended (what we call "cross-marketing"). Some of the more obvious choices (loss control, TPA services, disaster planning) will be discussed, with an eye toward obtaining maximum leverage from each of them. We'll also provide background and suggestions for developing "alternative market" sales in the risk financing areas, as well as how to establish and profit from association programs, risk retention groups and rent-a-captives.

This secondary theme will be pursued further into less traditional fields, suggesting that we be ready to sell employee leasing contracts, human resources services, business planning, general consulting, and "money products" like equipment leasing, venture capital, financing services, etc. So, non-insurance companies that are looking for better distribution systems for their non-insurance products would do well to read this book as an introduction to the P&C sales force and its advantages.

Selling and marketing activities are becoming more and more entwined with technology issues — sales force automation, database marketing, computer telephony integration, Internet and intranet utilization, presentation management, videoconferencing, groupware and collaborative software, etc. Where appropriate throughout our discussions, we will include information about current and developing technologies and how to select and use them for best advantage. In considering the future of the insurance sales industry, one eye must be kept on the future of technology, so an entire section of the book as well as an appendix is devoted to this specialty, and representatives from technology vendors may find, in these pages, new ideas about selling their products to insurance retailers.

Identifying a very broad "target audience" for this book is appropriate, because the marketplace, economic, and technological changes affecting us have broad and general influence. In one way or another, all groups named are connected in some way with the selling of insurance and related products and services. If you want to have your business sell more, and sell better, then this book is for you.

We think that the business world has changed so much that few, if any, will thrive by continuing to approach insurance sales and marketing the same way they did ten years ago. Of course, we don't have any monopoly on good ideas and tactics, so we have doubtless overlooked many successful strategies that might be applied. So, while any individual reader may use only some of the suggestions found here, we hope to have contributed to a more important change — a change in the way our business, and its future, is perceived. Our hope as authors is to induce a certain new mindset that will cause you to question, to explore, to innovate, and to expand beyond old, limiting horizons — venturing into broad new sales fields — using an approach, and taking advantage of tools, that would have been incredible just a few years ago.

Problems To Be Addressed

The P&C Retailer's Problems

While many of the categories of readers mentioned above work with and need to know about the P&C agent or broker, there are some special challenges and trends specifically threatening the P&C shop that will be expanded upon. Let's start with "the 3 Cs": Competition, Companies, and Consumers.

From the standpoint of the typical independent agent, they've seen the direct writing and captive agent companies tear a mighty piece out of "their" personal lines and small commercial market share. National brokers have lost business to the "alternative" marketplace and often play, at best, a support role in managing captives or providing ancillary captive-management services. "800 number" and Internet vendors are whittling away at the customer base of Allstate, State Farm and Nationwide. Large brokers and small agents are actively pursuing the "middle market" commercial accounts. Banks and brokerage houses are coming in, association programs drain away customers, and underwriting companies are battling hard for market share.

So while competition from every quarter lures your customers and battles you for prospects, the insurance companies aren't being much help.

They are playing a major role in the price-cutting seemingly-perpetual "soft market" that has dominated since the mid-80s. Forced to compete, they lower premiums. This lowers the commission of the agent or broker. On top of that, almost every company has cut into the commission percentage paid to the producer — so each sale that is won generates a smaller piece of a smaller pie than it would have just a few years ago.

Accelerating this downward-spiraling revenue whirlpool, as premiums are reduced, the likelihood of an underwriting profit goes with them — so chances for "contingency income" (profit sharing bonuses) dwindle from minuscule levels into obscurity. Increasingly fearful agency managers imagine company executives plotting: "And oh, by the way, we've just increased the minimum premium threshold for profit sharing, increased the stop-loss, and lowered the split — in case a statistical anomaly might have caused us inadvertently to have made a profit in your shop."

To compound the pressures, most companies have reduced their service staff ratio to business written, leaving the agent or broker to do more work, undertake more follow-up, and work harder for these reduced dollars they're earning. The agent's alternative to this increased workload seems to be to ignore the customer, who is besieged with competitive proposals.

So, the competition and the companies are making it a brutal environment for the agent and broker — which is bad enough. Then the phone rings, and your "special" customer has decided to "outsource" their risk management department, and (surprise, surprise!) you get to do some of their extra work! Your personal lines clients want appraisals and written summaries. Your BOP accounts want you to shop their account annually, and would move to a competitor for a $5 bill or a well-brewed cup of coffee. Your customers want answers, they want the right answers, and they want them now! They expect world-class efficiencies and responsiveness from your organization and everyone in the product stream.

These forces have combined to decimate net revenues and to demoralize the workforce in your shop — a talented group that sometimes appears ready to pack up and leave en masse. Everyone seems to be working harder for less.

We will show how to increase your revenues and profits per employee, per producer, per hour worked, per customer, per prospect, per sales call, and per owner. Implementing the systems and techniques in this book will make your P&C organization more attractive to clients and to talented producers (in the P&C as well as L&H specialties). These enhancements will increase the market value of your business and will generate satisfaction among your employees and customers. All in all, a fine package of results: should you choose to do the work and go through the changes needed to deliver it.

The L&H Retailer's Problems

Many of the difficulties mentioned above also apply to life sales professionals. In the once-lucrative term insurance field, rates and premiums have been reduced, and reduced again. Today, one can't spend much time with any media sources (TV, radio, magazine, newspaper, or the World Wide Web) without running across a pitch for the latest "term life superstore" with a toll-free number. These high-volume consolidators claim to automatically "quote from over 150 (or so) different insurance companies to get you the best deal possible." Term insurance has to a large extent become a commodity in the mind of consumers, who expect to obtain high limits at low cost with little hassle.

Today's life retailer has more competitors for the customers' dollars, from more financial products, than ever before. Mutual funds, money-market options, discount brokerages, and many other options entice the consumer to get the investment returns that, a while back, were available to most only through life products.

The financial services consumers today are much more sophisticated, and has many more options for access to the range of financial products, than did their counterparts even one or two decades ago. Whereas "whole life" products used to be a pillar of family financial planning, they are now considered as an afterthought (if at all). Go anywhere — the coffee shop, the bus stop, the supermarket — and you'll overhear talk of mutual funds, 401(k) plans, TSAs, commodity options, and more. Even in situations where life insurance might be the optimal product for a given situation, demonstrating that fact can be a major challenge. Modeling, for a demanding consumer, the behavior of a life product, and comparing it with other investment and protection alternatives, presents a major intellectual and technical challenge (see Chapter 7 for developments in this area).

Years ago, the P&C companies began "invading" the fields of life insurance, many of them developing strong product lines. For the one- or two-company life agent, this grew to be a source of frustration: often "independent" agents, with their ability to select from a half-dozen or more companies, could present very attractive and competitive proposals.

Regulators and legislators have, from their side, become more demanding as well. Replacement statutes and procedures, disclosure requirements, anti-churning laws, and stricter oversight have begun to take away most of the potential "short-cuts" to income from those who might have been inclined to use them. Like the P&C agent, the life agent must work harder, sell more, attend to more details, just to survive.

Cross-Selling, Cross Marketing, and Technology Utilization

Any introductory sales training course will teach the importance of "time and territory management" — encouraging salespeople to make several sales calls in the same area on the same day, find the best times of the week to make telephone calls, etc. — to make the best use of a precious and limited resource — selling time. Cross-selling (sales of additional lines of insurance to existing customers) and cross-marketing (offering services and solving client problems in areas that are beyond the scope of traditional insurance) bring time and territory management to another level. Cross-selling and cross-marketing activities eliminate waste and improve operating efficiencies on an organizational scale.

Effective cross-selling and cross-marketing programs will:

- Increase revenue per sales call
- Increase revenue per client relationship
- Reduce the market volatility arising from dependence on one or two product lines
- Improve client retention and keep the competition at bay
- Generate more fruitful referrals
- Improve relationships with existing carriers
- Attract coveted carrier relationships
- Attract energetic, ambitious producers to your sales force

Any good, experienced P&C producer will, on a new or renewal sales call, ask questions that probe for "insurance problems." After twelve or more years of "soft market" conditions, though, and with the growing sophistication of insurance buyers, producers on the street are finding that "insurance program design problems" are increasingly difficult to find. Most prospects have found their way to more or less the optimal underwriter for their account — an underwriter that understands them, an agent that coddles them, and a market that will price the heck out of the account every time outside competition appears.

The story is more common now than ever: producer after producer reports in after a day of sales calls, saying, "the only thing we can do to get that account is lower the price — and the incumbent is going to get the last chance to answer anything we come in with." No problems: no sales. "Hit ratios" are down, and frustration levels are up.

Now, imagine your producer on the same sales call, talking to a nice prospect, and instead of asking about "insurance problems," he or she could ask intelligent questions about "general business problems." When people today need to purchase a variety of goods, they head out to one of the big malls or a superstore — knowing that most of their buying needs will be met. The superstores have a better chance of selling something to everyone. And if producers are familiar with a whole suite of products and services, so that they can respond positively to today's problem, they are much more likely to make a sale and to please a customer. The producer doesn't have to be an expert in every product line, but needs to know enough to ask the right questions.

For help in "asking the right questions," we recommend Neil Rackham's classic, *SPIN Selling*. This primer provides a basic set of tools for any producer, directing them to probe, through skillful questioning, to identify the **S**ituation, uncover **P**roblems, lead the prospect to realize the **I**mplications of those problems, and lay bare the **N**eeds that lead to successful sales.

With training, if producers are confident that the agency has the expert on staff, or can bring in a top-quality and trusted outside vendor, and if producers share in the revenues generated from this expanded activity, then they will ask the questions. They will ask more regularly still if top agency management and sales management supports and encourages this activity with a firm commitment. With business needs now addressed, the customer, in turn, is much more likely to think of this producer when the next problem comes up. Through cross-selling and cross-marketing, a positive feedback cycle is set up, one that can help protect the relationship from outside competition.

To supplement this broader suite of products and the specialized training, a good sales organization needs to implement and take advantage of the technological tools available. This begins with powerful "agency management" software — to relieve a part of the "servicing" burden from the producer's back. But this is just the beginning. Further competitive advantage can arise from the systematic implementation of:

- Sales force automation (SFA) systems integrated with marketing programs
- Internet marketing and customer communications
- Electronic connections with underwriters and service providers
- Well-designed communications systems (cellular, voice mail, pagers, etc.)
- Professional looking (and sounding) presentation templates
- "Just in time" producer teaching and "Expert in a box" customer response capabilities
- Business planning and "opportunity response" systems

We'll talk about these and some other current and near-horizon technologies, and suggest how to develop an overall technology strategy and budget. As we proceed, we hope to develop a blueprint for the insurance sales organization of the near-future. It may look a bit strange to some, for it definitely departs from the older models. The idea of a Home Depot or Loew's building supply superstore would have been incredible to a hardware proprietor just twenty years ago. We anticipate changes as dramatic in the insurance retailing industry. The new agency, designed to take maximum advantage of existing assets, talents, and relationships, will sell many products and services, without losing the coherent mission and constant culture that will tie it all together. The prospect is exciting, the task is significant, and the rewards will be great.

Chapter 1

The Peaceful Past: Inertia and Relative Ease

We can imagine an astute member of the Board of Directors at Acme Buggy Whip, Inc., pounding his fist on the conference table during an annual meeting some 90 years ago, almost shouting, "First it was the passenger train! Now the consarned automobile! Why, before long, folks will probably be soaring around the skies in 'bird machines' or something! The writing is on the wall, gentlemen. Making a better buggy whip, or a prettier buggy whip, or a cheaper buggy whip is not the answer. We've got to make something that people will buy today and tomorrow."

Buggy whip manufacturers who defined themselves as "in the buggy whip business" died a quick and painful economic death. Those few who survived woke up to realize they were really in the "transportation enhancement" business; they went on to make steering cables, seat covers, convertible roofs and RV interiors. Many insurance retailers today still cling to the idea they are "in the insurance business," clinging to an outmoded sense of what that business really is. Such firms, whether large or small, venerable or newly formed, may be just tottering skeletons about to be blown over by the winds of economic change.

The Mid-Century Model: Agents and Brokers

To grow beyond old habits, it helps first to heighten our awareness of them. To characterize the old models of insurance retailing, let's take a look at the business as it was a few decades back. Yes, every form mentioned has undergone some change since then, but these changes have been, for the most part minor, incremental changes — cosmetic changes, if you will. Perhaps through reviewing how things used to be, with just a touch of exaggeration or caricature, we will see more clearly why some core elements of those models just aren't sustainable any more.

The American Agency System

Compared with today, independent agents and brokers lived in simpler times forty years ago. Policy forms were standardized and rarely changed, evolving at glacial paces. Rates were inflexible, permitting little opportunity for significant pricing advantage. Business was almost always placed locally, with an agent personally familiar with the customer. Competition from out of town was very rare. Family and business accounts remained loyal to "their" insurance agency for years, oftentimes for generations; People spoke of "my" insurance agent — and were about as likely to change agents as they were physicians. Corresponding demands could be heavy — a frequently-heard warning was, "I'm counting on you to cover me. I don't care what it is, I want to be covered."

While the battles between the local "mutual" agent and the local "stock" agent must have seemed of titanic proportions to those involved, there was really very little distinction between their products or the way they handled business. "Shopping" an account with any regularity would have been socially unacceptable. Commission rates of 25%, 30% or even 35% were the norm. "Loyalty" was a touchstone, and agents had companies they could count on, just as companies knew that their agents would toe the line when needed.

A hard-working insurance agent could expect to make a good living, and expected to make a little more the following year, by doing the same thing with the same clients in the same way. This constancy, which was a survival skill two generations ago, became an ingrained part of the culture at most P&C agencies. Innovation or radical change was likely to scare off more business than it could ever promise to attract.

The National Brokers

Back in the days when there were a dozen top-rung big brokers, "alphabet houses" were blissfully getting rich writing insurance policies for the Fortune 1000 and the larger shipping, mining, and energy businesses. Retrospectively rated casualty programs and engineered HPR property covers were the height of sophistication. Every once in a while a corporate treasurer would question the apparent conflict of interest involved in having an insurance advisor paid by commission, but this was considered "bad form." When pushed, the broker would grudgingly convert to a fee basis (often calculated by estimating what the commissions would have been, then "backing in" to that total by explaining how much his firm was worth).

One of the more important skills for the team leader on an account was business entertaining. If one could say right thing at dinner, play a decent (but not too good) round of golf, and hold up your end of the conversation in the fishing lodge, you made a difference in your firm's success. When it came to insurance, your client could choose national stock company "A," say the Hartford, or national stock company "B," perhaps the Aetna — but their forms and rates were close to indistinguishable. Self-insurance was rarely considered, let alone offshore captives. Big accounts were fun, and there were plenty to go around — let the independent agents take care of the smaller accounts.

The Life Agent and Life MGA

Fifty years ago, every little town in the United States had its own "life insurance man" (and yes, he was a man). This life agent represented one company, and sold a half-briefcase full of simple products modeled on the traditional fixed premium whole life or aggregate rate convertible and renewable term life chassis. First-year commissions were high, renewal commissions were in the 5% range. Life agents talked of retirement based upon a block of existing "permanent" business renewals. When prospects were healthy, they got their insurance; if they were sick, they were usually declined coverage. If the agent sold enough, he and his wife got to go on a company-sponsored trip to a nearby city or resort.

The battle of the day was the struggle between mutual and stock company agents. Dividends in a stock life insurance policy were almost as predictable as a train schedule. There was enough "fat" in the product to meet or exceed projected dividends year in and year out for most stock carriers. As purveyors of "non-participating insurance" mutual agents suggested that clients should "buy non-par and invest the difference" rather receive a belated "refund of an overcharge," which is how the mutual agent described a stock dividend.

Except for the period surrounding the Armstrong investigation (which established non-forfeiture provisions and put caps on agent commissions) around the turn of the century, "regulation" of the life insurance industry over the last hundred years ago was for the most part a "sleepy" business. One could barely manage a life company badly enough to run it into the ground, so regulators weren't under a lot of pressure to be "watchdogs." The job of state insurance commissioner was often a "cushy" political appointment, requiring more the ability to endure endless banquets than any skill at accounting. Relations between the insurance department and the agents they were supposed to be regulating was mostly amiable, at times even cozy.

A career as a "life agent" was viewed by many as a "calling" — carrying out the obviously altruistic work of protecting future widows and orphans from poverty and despair. Top life agents were highly visible people within their communities, participating in fraternal, civic, and charitable organizations. With little negative media focus, the life agent was admired; media questions regarding the life product's competitive value or intrinsic worth were never heard. No one criticized the life agent's or company's marketing practices.

Being a life insurance general agent (GA) back then almost guaranteed one the "good life." Recruiting new agents was a pretty enjoyable business. While the ultimate "success rate" for new producers was not much better than today, life companies were willing to support the "body count" method, just to continue bringing in the few pieces of new business that even a mediocre recruit could generate. Recruiting bonuses for GAs were based upon the number of new recruits, with little attention being paid to actual new production.

And Along Came A Spider... State Farm and Allstate

There were just too many inefficiencies in the distribution systems outlined above, and too much money flowing through them, not to invite new competitors with "streamlined" business models. The "captive agent" alternatives, as exemplified by State Farm, recognized and took advantage of the opportunities of the day. One might say that these companies "suburbanized" the retail insurance business — identifying and seeking out the profitable middle-class "cream" business. State Farm designed their distribution system around this growing, affluent sector, and as a result, gained market share rapidly.

As the population became more mobile and more "brand" conscious, State Farm created a national, brand-name presence. As one of the first to recognize the power of cross-selling in retaining customers, State Farm made life insurance an "equal partner" with the homeowners and automobile lines. Training their agents in the technical and selling sides of all three lines, State Farm (and Allstate, and some others) soon pulled significant market share away from the independent P&C shop, and even drew some life sales away from old-style life agency systems. Circumventing the regional field offices, cumbersome redundancies, and poorly-designed workflows of the national stock and mutual companies, these upstarts rocketed to market shares of around 40% in just a couple of decades.

To a great extent, though, even these "new" approaches carried forward some of the baggage of the system they hoped to replace. These new insurance companies, like the national stock and regional mutual firms that preceded them, continued to view themselves as product generators, and focused their retail distribution on processes. A typical cycle would involve the company creating property and casualty and/or life insurance products designed to meet certain identifiable market niches. They would then recruit and train agents to be able to identify such prospects, whose "profile" indicated they had needs their products would fit, and then the agents would go out and sell them.

Under this "product or process-centric" strategy, companies sold what they had to sell and consumers bought what was offered or went to another company. Later on, we will contrast this with a "client-centric" strategy, one that starts with the existing client or prospect's needs and wishes (even those outside of the client's current awareness), and then builds a sales system and a product line around those specific needs. For now, we'll just point out that all of these market segments (independent P&C and life agents, brokers, and "captive agency" vendors) generated their sales through a system that was highly segmented, very regulated, and not very automated.

Obstacles to Cross-Selling

The advances made by State Farm and Allstate did point out one abiding truth — the more (lines) you have to sell to a prospect, the more likely you are to sell him *something*. The corollary to this became clear to all: the more (lines) you actually sell to a client, the more likely they are to remain a customer. Cross-selling is not only a door-opener, it also helps to secure the long-term loyalty of a customer.

Many traditional agency retailers, fearing the loss of even more precious market share, decided to try doing something about it. "Let's set up a life department" became the frequently-intoned mantra among independent P&C agents, while many life-only agents sought to form alliances with the P&C shop down the street. It turned out, though, not to be so easy. Experiments of all types were tried, and many of them either failed miserably or died a slow, painful death. Today's agent can learn from these past experiments, and by recognizing the inherent problems involved in expanding sales program into new product lines, can better prepare his or her cross-selling and cross-marketing plans for the future.

One way to analyze past obstacles and barriers would be by looking at different size P&C operations, since the impediments differ somewhat between smaller and larger retailers. We can then consider psychological, cultural, management, and industry structural issues.

Barriers Specific to Small P&C Agencies

As recently as the 1970s, the retail P&C insurance industry was dominated (by number of agencies) by "small" agencies producing $1,500,000 or less in annual premiums. Such shops were typically made up of one owner, one to three "secretaries," and perhaps a junior "owner in training," and a younger producer busy trying to figure out how to "sell." These agencies usually had a very strong, long-standing relationship with one or two "lead" companies, with whom they placed most of their business. A few other contracted markets and a variety of excess and surplus lines wholesalers were kept around to pick up the pieces that didn't fit in with the lead carriers.

Simple as the above model appears on the surface, the business life of the agency itself was often hectic and complex. Such an agency typically insured one or two in almost every segment of the economy — a paint store, a lumber yard, a library, a metal shop, a clinic, etc. This meant that the staff had to become somewhat of an expert in each of these business areas. Coverage options, enhancements, and available endorsements had become many and varied, so a high level of technical expertise was expected. If the agency made any serious errors, two or three competitors were waiting right down the street to show the client that they could do a better job.

Additionally, more than half the smaller agent's time was taken up with dealing with personal lines P&C business, making auto change endorsement requests, quoting on homeowner's policies, and responding to a claims problem involving his best customer's teenage son.

The general state of affairs was that the small agent had too many balls in air and could never seem to find time to mention life insurance as an option. Life insurance appeared to be another discipline, another specialty, that would require time and effort to learn and even more time to master. The resources just weren't available to undertake the task.

In recent decades, a certain impetus came from the P&C companies anxious themselves for life insurance to be sold by their agents. Any number of companies established, acquired, or enhanced life divisions, understanding that there was money to be made there and that they had a sales force "ready made," if they could be motivated. While over the course of many years a number of these P&C life divisions did achieve considerable size (and did contribute substantially to the bottom line of their parent companies), nevertheless it was slow going for the most part. Many strategies were implemented to speed up this growth — trips, enhanced commissions, stepped-up P&C profit sharing bonuses, and veiled (or real) threats regarding minimum life production. It would be fair to say, though, that results from these efforts rarely lived up to the companies' more optimistic expectations.

A definite obstacle to these life product development efforts from P&C companies, particularly in early years, was that the products themselves were not competitive. Startup ventures in any major line of insurance are often at a marketplace disadvantage: reinsurance costs are higher when there is no track record, underwriting expertise must be imported, assumptions must be conservative, and only a few basic products can be rolled out at one time. So, small agents trying to sell their P&C company's new life offerings were often embarrassed with their customers — only a little "shopping around" would reveal just how lacking in features and high-priced their proposals were. Used to being the best at what they did, many agents quickly dropped life sales activities and returned to their strengths.

Life insurance sales did not, for the most part, become a standard part of the small agency's way of doing business. When it came to estate planning, business needs life planning, and other medium-level life insurance challenges, the small agent felt out of his league. The potential life customer was aware of this, and usually preferred going to the "life-only specialist" for all but the most elementary life insurance needs. Many consumers were unlikely to think of their P&C agent when it came to their life insurance needs.

Even the local State Farm and Allstate agents have disappointed, as a group, their employers as life producers. After all, these companies were designed from the ground up to offer all of the critical insurance coverages to every customer — "Auto, Home, and Life." To the extent that they succeeded, we can still learn from them. Top executives at any of these firms will admit, however, that their system should be selling a lot more, and that they are missing many opportunities to "tie up" their customers through total account selling.

Barriers Obstructing Larger Retailers

P&C agencies in bigger towns and cities grew, out of necessity, beyond the scale of the small-town shops. Even in the more suburban and rural areas the smaller shops began closing down, merging, or acquiring one another. As a result of these trends, a shift in market dominance began which continues today — a shift toward mid-size agencies with revenues ranging from $2 million to $5 million. Despite their size, the same types of time constraints and prospect perception have slowed down the growth of life sales in the larger retail shops as well.

There have been some additional barriers to cross-selling that can be identified. Until a few years ago, big P&C retailers were licensed, not only to sell insurance, but also (it seems in retrospect) to print money. That is, the agency business was widely profitable and generated significant rewards for the owners and their top producers. Success, while it provides resources for change and growth, also breeds inertia. "Don't mess with success" was a motto that fit in very nicely with the conservative culture and established background of many large agencies. When revenues and profits were high, motivation to take on new sales and management programs was low.

Another obstruction was the territoriality of individual producers and their support teams. With larger accounts generating tens of thousands of dollars of revenue year after year, every producer's biggest fear was losing the account, and one of the few ways to lose an account back then was to make a big mistake in handling part of it. Such a mistake would attract the attention and invite the ire of the client. In light of this fear, a natural defense was to try exerting maximum control over the situation. So the thought processes would run something like this: "I can control my own action, and I can manage my team, and I can try to browbeat my underwriting companies, because I have some clout there. However, I can't count on controlling anything else — so 'anything else' is to be excluded."

As a result, producers objected strongly to the introduction of any other departments or products to "his" client. When explicit objections didn't work, concerned producers found a variety of ways to sabotage cross-marketing efforts. This "mentality of the fiefdom" lives on in many guises in the larger retail shops even today.

Yesterday's larger agencies had their roots in smaller agencies. As discussed above, the core identity of most of these old-time small shops was that of a P&C agency. This identity carried forward in time, whereby the business itself was intimately connected with the product that it sold. It would have required a very deep-seated series of changes to have altered this identity. Consequently, to have seriously pursued the sale of life insurance would have been almost as upsetting as would selling shoes have been.

Even where the will and the vision was present, automation and sales process systems had not yet been developed that would have made cross-selling or cross-marketing as efficient as it has become today. The ability to generate and "mine" customer information from agency databases or to track prospects and customers through time with sales force automation (SFA) tools simply did not exist or were unaffordable back then.

Still another barrier to cross-selling activity was an ironic "can't see the trees for the forest" problem: commercial producers sold "accounts." Ask a producer where he was heading, the likely response would have been "I'm going over to ABC Wholesalers, Inc." It is almost too obvious to point out, that a corporation is a "person" only in the eyes of the law. The producer, though, saw the corporation as his customer. However, life insurance has as its subject only natural persons — a life policy covers the life of a human being. Selling to individual human beings at a corporation was in some way unnatural — it didn't fit in with the accustomed rhythm of a business sales call. L&H sales imply face to face, human to human interactions, not the human to company or company to company outlook that has become habitual in the outlook of P&C people. This suggests psychological differences at work, which we explore more in the next section.

Even the jumbo regional and national brokers have had their problems taking advantage of cross-selling opportunities. While their clients are composed of the largest employers in the country, a national broker's life insurance client list is nowhere near as extensive. The "alphabet houses" would focus on battering each other in competition for the P&C business of the Fortune 1000, and everything else faded into the background as a less-than-serious business goal. We will see later that the national brokers have led the way in the insurance industry when it comes to the cross-marketing of many non-life insurance services, but their successes in life-only sales have been more limited.

So, even among those retailers that do sell some life insurance, these efforts have often been an afterthought. One might almost describe L&H sales activities in most shops as an "accommodation" to demanding customers or companies, or as a "hobby" for the unusually productive producer.

General Cultural and Psychological Barriers

Compared with full-time life salespeople, full-time P&C agents are more combative, or one might say, more gleefully competitive. The typical, "plain vanilla" life insurance sale might be described as a "win-win-win" situation, in that a new product is sold (presumably to meet a need, so the customer wins), where none existed before (so that the selling agent and the underwriting company also win): no losers here. Yes, "replacement" sales do occur (more than the companies like to admit), but the replaced agent loses only a relatively insignificant renewal commission.

Contrast this with almost any P&C sale, wherein one retailer takes a customer away from another. The customer, presumably, has benefited, or he would not have changed. The new agent and company are also pleased. However, very much in the context of this sales dynamic, there is also someone who has lost — the former agent and company. A P&C sale might thus be thought of as a win-win-lose scenario. Churning and switching of companies and brokers is the rule, rather than the exception on the P&C side. "What's your ex-date?" and "Let me see if I can get a better value on your renewal" are the oft-sung refrains of most P&C producers.

When a successful P&C agent hears that one of their competitors has suffered a loss, the typical reaction is a delighted chortle. In announcing the successful closing of a new account to the agency, a P&C agent is as likely to say, "We got another one away from Brown and Brown," as she is to report just on her success. Most P&C producers will grin happily even if some other competitor steals business from their main competitor — "The enemy of my enemy is my friend."

On the other hand, when most life agents make a sale they are likely to talk about how they helped the client, or how they convinced the underwriter to remove a "rating." Even when "replacing" another company's product, the life agent is required in most jurisdictions to fill out comparison forms and to carefully explain the advantages to the customer of making the change. Even the word "replacing" is so innocuous-sounding that it is never heard on the P&C side of the business — perhaps because almost every P&C sale is in fact a "replacement." P&C agents grab accounts from competitors and then hang on to them tooth and nail — they don't "replace" anything.

The fact that another underwriting company might be losing a customer is very much in the background of the life sales transaction; and the other retail agent appears to be losing very little indeed. This leads to another difference in product psychology, which arises from the traditional commission structure of the two industries. Life sales have been typically compensated with a very high front-end commission, which reduces drastically, sometimes to zero, at renewal. A P&C producer, in contrast, is rewarded for their sale year after year on a more or less "level" basis.

Non-level commissions also mean that, to survive, the life agent must in fact be a salesperson — they must sell something new, usually to someone new, week after week, year after year. In most industries, good salespeople are among the best-compensated employees, often earning more than top executives in the company. This is because selling almost any product is usually very hard work: it requires considerable training (and polishing of that training), and it requires a rather rare set of personal qualities and characteristics.

The attrition rate among novice life producers is extremely high compared with almost any other industry. In contrast, many P&C agents in the past had found what amounted to a life of relative ease, in which they have been paid quite a lot to do what amounted to very little — "After all, most of the accounts keep renewing, so why knock yourself out?" In other words, while P&C agents have managed to keep busy, many of them haven't had to do the hard work of selling, at least not after they established a book of business. In this sense, the P&C agent's primary outlook has been defensive, to maintain what they already have, while the life agent has constantly had to be on the offensive, going after more new customers with energetic tenacity.

L&H products, including disability income, are viewed by the buying public as discretionary products, "nice to have," if affordable. One rarely needs life insurance to get a car loan, or even to buy a home. Contrast this with P&C personal lines as well as commercial insurance, which are viewed as more "mandatory" in nature. No home or car loan can be secured without them, few businesses would consider running without a good P&C program for protection. In fact, the law of the land sometimes requires P&C insurance — in order to register a car, for instance, or for a business to have any employees (workers compensation coverage).

These differences in customer and producer outlook arose in large part from differences in the products themselves. These product differences are much greater between Life and P&C than are the differences between, say, commercial P&C and personal lines P&C. It is the rule, rather than the exception, to see retail shops that are split 60/40 or 70/30, one way or the other, between personal and commercial P&C revenues.

It is very rare indeed to find a retailer with such a balance between P&C and L&H lines. One might at first glance think that cross-selling L&H has to be pretty similar to cross-selling personal lines, but this is not the case.

The subject matter of the two product lines also produce distinct psychological reactions in the customer. There is a big difference, emotionally, between considerations of one's death and contemplating the loss of a piece of property. Death, after all, seems to mean the loss of everything in this world. It is of ultimate significance to the person — all other loss pales in comparison. Ensuring that one's home can be repaired after a windstorm is sensible and conservative; dying, on the other hand, is an almost unimaginable act — difficult at best to talk about. The sales process for life insurance must then be quite a bit different than for P&C.

The Psychology of the Life Insurance Sale

Life insurance, an intangible product, is for the most part an emotional purchase. You can't eat or drink, drive, or touch life insurance — the need for it must be *felt*. To paraphrase what Georgia State professor Stuart Schwartzchild once said, "Large amounts of life insurance will not be bought out of any economic necessity...like diamonds, large amounts will be bought only out of love." Now this may be love of family, love of a business or care for employees, love of an alma mater or favorite charity or institution, or simply love of oneself.

To generate a major life insurance sale the agent must produce a vivid portrait, in the mind and emotions of the prospect, of what life insurance can do for the loved one. It is the skill in eliciting this feeling and arousing a desire to benefit any or all of these parties that must be "painted" in vibrant emotional "colors," by the life salesperson.

This ability to connect emotionally with the life prospect requires an inherent skill — the ability to observe and to listen with extreme sensitivity. Even this observation and listening cannot be just random activity — after all, there are only so many hours in the month, and several sales must be made. Accordingly, the life producer must also be skilled at directed questioning, a process whereby the prospect is led, by providing their own answers, to uncover their own deepest concerns and their most tender altruistic goals. This leads to an increased awareness in the prospect's own mind, of their own personal loves — which in turn leads ultimately to the life sale.

Such talk about love and emotion can seem very strange to those of us who are more "analytical" by nature (including many P&C people). However, the failure of P&C management to understand and accept life's more "emotional nature of the decision to buy" will hamstring life sales efforts within that agency. A P&C producer trying to sell life products will never evolve beyond an "order-taker" in the life business without this sensitivity and these skills. Old-style P&C people are now used to dealing with insurance as commodity, and have become habituated to responding without thought to requests to find the cheapest solution in the shortest amount of time.

Not that "order taking" is necessarily all bad: even if you or your agency don't wish to go beyond this mentality, there is still plenty of life business to be written, especially for retailers who adopt a more organized, automated, and efficient system. But, if your agency expects to unearth, cut, and polish the large potential "diamonds" that are out there in life sales, your managers and producers must recognize and deal with the emotional nature of the big life sale.

A psychological aspect common to both to large and small life situations is the tendency of the prospect to procrastinate. Many people will put off, literally forever, the purchase of life insurance, unless they are reminded and re-reminded of the need until they are prodded into taking action. This is a very different situation from the typical P&C sale, and requires special training and a different design in the specific selling sequences involved.

The dogged persistence of the successful life insurance agent can seem foreign, if not reprehensible, to the P&C agent. This persistence is nonetheless necessary. For a P&C agent (or a bank) to achieve success in the marketing of life insurance, where such attributes are not psychologically innate, an automated sales system will likely be required, one that forces the frequent, recurrent, persistent "bugging" of the prospect. Another alternative would be to bring in people that do have this "life mentality," and then support and work with them.

At any given time, many of the individuals that are P&C clients, or who work for commercial P&C clients, do in fact need life insurance (whether they are aware of it or not). Since the P&C agent is already talking with these people, and has established a degree of trust with them, to ignore these needs could be thought of as a great waste. Dozens of "golden opportunities" in the life area are waiting to be uncovered by someone and it might as well be you (or your firm). The psychological accommodations required to make the life sale may generate a certain amount of discomfort for the agent, but the rewards for following through will be more than commensurate.

Management Skills and Management Time

Because of the previosuly mentioned differences, managers at P&C retailers have some extra challenges facing them as they move the organization to seriously expand into L&H sales. We've already talked about the resistance to be expected from the P&C production force, protecting their "territory," working defensively to keep "their" accounts from being messed up. To overcome this kind of resistance requires a real commitment from the very top, so that everyone in the organization understands that the transition to broader product lines will happen, and that opposition, whether overt or subtle, will not be tolerated.

This commitment carries with it certain necessary consequences which require management to review almost every aspect of their operation and to make a number of seemingly extensive changes. To evolve L&H sales efforts beyond the "order taking" stage, hard decisions must be made in many areas, including resource allocation, employee compensation, recruiting and training, automation, strategic partnerships, and relationships with vendors. In Chapters 3 through 6 we will go into what is required to make these changes and give detailed suggestions for bringing L&H sales to a much higher level in your shop.

If the only result of all this effort were the increased revenues and profit available, the work to be done will make sense to many retailers. However, there is only so much time available to top management, and there are many other promising projects that beckon. However, precisely because L&H sales are so different from P&C activities, and because so many changes must be instituted to incorporate a powerful L&H sales presence, a hidden advantage will begin to appear for those that undertake the task. Those retailers who redesign their operation for L&H, will already have done most of the work required to incorporate sales of many other products and services to the same customers and prospects during the same sales calls. This redesign and reorganization isn't something that must be done over and over for every new product the agency gets an opportunity to sell. As we will see in Chapter 6 on the cross-marketing of other products and services, the L&H system is scalable and adaptable to other kinds of revenue opportunities.

Chapter 2

Winds of Change

This book wouldn't have been written if P&C retailers were as fat and happy now as they were twenty years ago. Obviously, things have changed; while the pace of change has been so rapid as to make the fact of this change transparent, we would do well to examine a few major components of our business situation through the lens of these changes themselves. Most changes follow one another in a certain sequence, and point in the general direction that becomes our future. By studying some of these indicators, we will uncover some clues about the paths that lead to success, as well as some signals warning us about the more perilous routes for the coming years.

Societal and Demographic Changes

First, and perhaps foremost, it would be easy to overlook change and the pace of that change, as one of these indicators. That tomorrow's business environment will be significantly different from today's can be stated with certainty. Like biological organisms, organizations are interdependent with their environment: when one changes, the other necessarily adapts, or dies. Accordingly, any business hoping to thrive in the next few years must have provisions for these changes built into its operating plan. We know that changes of many sorts will be requisite — just what those changes will be is a different matter. The point here is, if your organization is not aggressively undertaking change as a way of life, its future is bleak.

In the Introduction, we discussed the "three C's": Competition, Companies and Consumers. Here we'll talk about them a bit more, in the context of transformations involving them. Consumers now are more sophisticated in business and more demanding. They know that they have many choices when it comes to P&C insurance, and have learned that the exercise of choice has been leading them to lower pricing, better coverage, and more satisfying service response. Even when commercial P&C buyers are pretty happy where they are, they know that "getting a couple quotes" can do them little harm, and will likely get them better terms on their renewal. As long as the threat to move their business is somewhat serious, producers live in constant peril. Renewal commissions, after all, have been the P&C retailer's lifeblood.

The days of earning robust commissions on huge policy premiums are fading fast. When corporate insurance budgets approach six figures, more and more questions are being asked. The buyer wants to know how much of their premium goes to compensate the retailer, and what the retailer is actually doing to earn such amounts. Trying to answer questions like these in a way that will satisfy a tough-minded corporate controller has embarrassed more than one producer. The bigger an account, the more we can expect a demand to convert from commissions to fees — and fee-based compensation requires that we provide work worth paying us for, and that we document this work carefully.

We often hear that our economy is becoming more and more an international one, and that competitors can arise from any part of the globe. This seems to have been more the case in manufacturing, so far, than it has been in insurance. Everyone can see the impact that European, Japanese, and Korean automobile manufacturing has had on the "Big Three" US suppliers. Overseas competition provided a wake-up call that got Ford, GM and Chrysler working harder and smarter, building better products and servicing them at a level that would have been unbelievable three decades ago.

The demands of international markets have been less obvious in the insurance business so far, and are not as far along in their evolutionary impact on United States retailing. This is due partly to the fact that insurance, as an intangible "financial" problem, is less obviously either foreign or domestic. Reinsurance dollars, for instance, could be thought of as fungible goods. However, the fact that international insurance and financial organizations are in fact playing a much greater role in the insuring of US risks has meant that products are developed faster, with more features, and at lower costs than would otherwise be the case.

The globalization of our economy has another implication — that our customers are more involved in importing, exporting, and travel abroad than ever before. If retailers do not anticipate and meet the insurance and related needs that arise out of these exposures, then savvier competitors surely will.

Our customers and prospects are more accustomed than ever to expecting convenience when they shop, whether this means finding every kind of good at a mall or receiving advice on every kind of investment from their stock broker. Because our lives are so full and hectic, we expect "everywhere, anytime" options for our routine transactions, and will pay extra for this kind of convenience. In offering this kind of breadth in options, our competitors are, paradoxically, becoming more and more focused. They know that they must be true experts to sell big-ticket products and services today.

Corporations themselves look and act differently nowadays, and the pace of this change is evolving rapidly. Many traditional corporate functions are outsourced, sometimes even to "competitors." At the same time, businesses form and dissolve all manner of alliances, joint ventures, and "partnerships" that can respond quickly to pressing needs or brief opportunities, with a minimal commitment of resources from the parties involved. Mergers and acquisitions are the order of the day. Yesterday's Fortune 100 are today's history lessons.

In the United States, and to varying degrees in other countries, people are more inclined than ever to "shift the blame" for their personal and economic problems onto society at large (through social welfare programs) or onto purported wrongdoers (through litigation). Even recent welfare and tort reform movements must be considered in the context of the much wider movement that they are in reaction to. These movements have implications for the insurance industry in areas such as retirement planning, agents' professional liability ("E&O"), long-term care product sales, and others. Certainly, if the public expects the insurance retailer to let them know what they need, the retailer had better know about and had better consistently recommend a wide variety of protection.

Technological Changes

Societal and demographic changes are interwoven with, and mutually reinforced by, developments in technology. Even a partial listing of the innovations in computers and communications over the past two decades suggests how deep the accompanying changes have been in buying patterns, company relationships, and competitive pressures. Consider the impact of fax machines, cell phones, scanners, digital cameras, local- and wide-area networks, the Internet, personal computers, voicemail, applications software, agency management software, and e-mail.

Because of the power and the pervasive integration of these tools, the old ways of business just don't work any more. Also, because more information can be handled and used by technology-savvy companies, new opportunities to sell can be identified and exploited. We'll delve into these opportunities in Chapter 7.

The most powerful and "cutting edge" technology is often affordable only for comparatively large organizations. This has been one of the driving forces behind mergers and consolidations at all levels of the insurance industry: the recognition of the competitive advantages available with implementation of the latest systems. Smaller retailers sometimes cannot afford to purchase, learn, and use many of these powerful tools. Many are so complex as to require an in-house expert for full utilization.

However, there is a countervailing, and paradoxical effect at work at the same time: because of technology, the smaller operations can now do what only the large shops could handle a few years back. Electronic communication with vendors and clients, presence on the World Wide Web, production of attractive color presentations, and instant rating are just a few of these abilities that have trickled down to the smallest retailers. This trend will continue to expand geometrically, as the cost of ever-more-powerful systems continues to plummet. Small size implies increased flexibility, and it will be easier, at certain price points, for the very small shop to jump into the latest systems, while large, bureaucratic organizations will have a hard time overhauling their complex, inter-dependent systems.

For existing retailers and companies there is the overriding long-term threat that someone will design new product delivery systems from the ground up that are centered around the latest technology. Many of these systems will not make compromises for or be compatible with "legacy systems" already in use. Adoption of these new systems may threaten long-time employees who have "always done it the old way" and are reluctant to change.

Another reason the speed of technological change has been under-appreciated is the small percentage of the current power structure that is computer literate. There are some that feel very threatened by this impending revolution and actually want to slow its approach down until they've retired.

Industry Trends

Retailers working in the insurance business must change not only because society, their customers, and technology are changing but because of the metamorphosis of the insurance business itself — the context in which we work. On both the L&H and the P&C sides, there has been considerable consolidation at every level of the industry; companies acquire other companies, brokers merge with other brokers, agencies "cluster" together, and affinity organizations have grown in relative importance. New or redesigned products are introduced regularly. New competitors arise from wholly-unexpected directions. New distribution systems are being rolled out regularly. As a foundation for strategic planning, we'll consider these, and other, developments in some detail for both the P&C and for the L&H retailing industries.

P&C Industry Developments

We heard a producer in a large agency joking that they had an office pool based on which would come first: the next hard market, or the next Ice Age. Like most jokes, this one contains more than a grain of truth — the insurance "market" will never again go through the same predictable gyrations that identified it for generations. The market itself has mutated as the driving technologies have advanced, and the economic context in which insurance products are "traded" seems to expand and deepen almost daily.

For more than a decade, in almost every line of insurance in the United States, gross premiums per unit of exposure have been declining (total written premiums have edged up in most lines from year to year, but not as rapidly as the insured economy has grown). There are three underlying causes, and none of them is tied to the old "underwriting cycle;" they are the demands for efficiency, reduced losses, and investment income.

The Drive for Efficiency

Every participant in the insurance delivery system is battling to become more efficient. The expense portion of each insurance dollar is declining and (as uncomfortable as this is sure to make the reader) there is a lot more available to be pared out as efficiencies that are forced by the marketplace improve. This driving force is just a subset of the larger international competitive trend that challenges every industry. It is augmented by the relative ease with which capital may be committed to insurance (basically, by filing a few documents and writing a check, in contrast to building a $2 billion chip fabrication plant). For the foreseeable future, if there is even the appearance of an opportunity in insurance, dollars (and other forms of currency) will rush in. If you are not making money in insurance today you are in trouble. Sorry to say, though, if you are making money, look out! It won't take long for your competitors to find a way to squeeze you out.

Just as many regional and branch offices of insurance companies have been closed down to cut costs, these international forces, coupled with consumer expectations, will force our business to consolidate vertically even more. "Disintermediation" will be the call of the future — getting rid of the layers of our business that connect the customers to the final value they seek. Some survivors (call them "company-centric") will find ways to eliminate the agent, others ("agent-centric") will discover that insurance companies (as they are traditionally organized) are an unnecessary luxury. The bold fact, though, is that for most types of insurance you don't need an agent, company branch office (or wholesaler), or a company home office to connect the consumer with the reinsurance wealth of the world, or even to provide the answers and assistance desired by the consumer.

All that will be required is one, almost seamless and very efficient distribution and communication system. The functions that in the past have been undertaken by agents and companies will continue to be performed, but without the hand-offs, redundancies, and friction that impair even the best models today.

Retailers (agencies) that wish to survive long-term as significant entities would be well advised to identify, cultivate relationships with, and/or create insurance or reinsurance companies that are willing to fade into the background, efficiently providing just a few necessary functions like product development and filing, claims management, and underwriting direction. Cincinnati Insurance Company, formed a few decades ago by insurance agents, was visionary in this respect. To this day, the Cincinnati has no branch offices, no heavy infrastructure, and relies heavily on the front-line, relationship-based underwriting and processing capabilities of their carefully-selected agencies. A more recent evolutionary step in this direction can be seen in Mutual Risk Management, whose subsidiaries Commonwealth Risk and Legion Insurance Company provide turnkey rent-a-captives to agencies through their "Agency Profit Center" and similar programs.

Insurance companies wishing to predominate should, in contrast, look for ways to relegate the retailer to a low-paid, high-volume sales-only function (much as Progressive Insurance Co. has done) or to bypass the agent completely through 800-number, Internet, or other direct sales channels (such as GEICO and USAA).

Improvements in Controlling Losses

A second force squeezing premiums is the decline in actual losses and loss costs per unit of exposure. Tort law reform, safety engineering, fraud prevention, claims management, WC reform, safer autos and machinery, drug and alcohol testing, adherence to building codes, better product engineering and quality, societal awareness, and other factors all play their part, and all reinforce one another. About two-thirds to three-quarters of the insurance dollar today goes to pay claims, so when claims are less frequent and less severe, fewer premium dollars are required.

It has long been proclaimed that the insurance industry plays an important social role — that of increasing safety consciousness and preventing losses. The long-term effects of doing this well are that, paradoxically, insurance isn't called upon as often, relative to the number of exposures covered, as it used to be. The larger a commercial client becomes, typically, the more resources (proportionally) they can commit to loss control and safety engineering. Once the true cost of claims becomes apparent to an organization's top management, they start doing something about controlling those costs. Over time, such programs have effect, loss history improves, and insurance costs go down. This usually means that revenues for the retailer go down as well.

The Impact of Investment Income

A third factor holding down insurance premiums is the healthy and gradually expanding worldwide economy, which has provided vigorous growth in investment income for the insurance industry, reinforcing the cash flows from underwriting. The American stock market, through mid-1997 had been through the longest, steadiest boom in its history. Bonds have been affordable. Even a downturn in stocks and bonds won't keep today's sophisticated insurance company investment managers from finding viable alternatives in the international markets. In this context, making an "underwriting profit" can appear to be a waste of resources, when the potential growth from the "float" is taken into account. By cutting the rates just a bit more, the reasoning goes, market share can be increased, so more total dollars will be rolling in and available for company investment.

This healthy economy has also been in a reinforcing feedback relationship with the decline of losses and loss costs — the decline in losses per unit of exposure. Because of a stable, growing economy, corporate and family insureds have been able to repair, maintain, and buy new vehicles, plants and machinery — and these newer, better-designed items are inherently safer than old, worn-out, "maintenance-deferred" buildings and equipment.

Factors could (and at some time likely will) intrude to mitigate some of these effects for a short period of time — a string of weather-related or geological catastrophes could hammer loss ratios for a while or the worldwide economy could stall or decline. These eventualities are not likely to divert the underlying trends, however. The insurance industry is being forced to become increasingly more efficient, less costly, than it used to be — and that means premiums (and the commissions based on them) will continue to grow more slowly than the economy.

So, we have the typical P&C retailer squeezed in a very uncomfortable "triple-whammy" — premiums are down, the percentage of that lower premium is declining, and companies are targeting a 100% or higher combined ratio — which means no underwriting profit and no profit sharing bonus for the retailer.

The Shrinking Pie

While gross insurance premiums stagnate or decline, the alternatives to traditional insurance draw portions of the purchasing public away from the P&C agency every year. In the 1960s and '70s independent agencies (and their companies) stood by while direct writers carried away a huge portion of their personal lines book — often "skimming the cream" of the best, most profitable risks. In recent years, a market share balance seems to have been struck between independents and the captive agent and direct writing insurers. However, at the same time, even newer marketing options like direct mail, "800 number," kiosk, and Internet alternatives continue the assault on the P&C agent's book.

While the State Farms and Allstates were battering down the personal lines front door, another threat crept through the commercial lines bushes out back. This threat was not immediately obvious; in fact, for a long time, it seemed only to affect the gigantic accounts of the largest national brokers. What P&C agent took the time to worry about "self insurance," offshore "captive" insurance companies, pooling operations, "paid loss retrospective plans" or other esoteric developments? These arrangements were playthings of the Fortune 100, and would never be appropriate for the middle market accounts paying our bills. Or would they?

If your agency is typical, in the last five years you have lost more than one of your key commercial accounts to the "alternative market." We've almost all received that dreaded phone call, or had that disastrous meeting, during which the bomb was dropped: "We love the way you've serviced our account for the past thirty years, but this deal was just too attractive for us to ignore. We're going to join the XYZ municipality pool (or the ABC rent-a-captive, or we're going to self-insure our malpractice exposures)." Depending on how it is measured, approximately 40% of U.S. commercial risk exposures are now underwritten and financed through the "alternative market."

Other commercial and personal lines customers of the traditional agencies have found that they can get broader coverage and lower price for insurance products through an association or group of some kind. Any retailer of any size has lost more than one business customer who placed their insurance with the state's funeral directors association program or something similar. We all know of people who now get their auto or home insurance "direct" through the AARP or some other regional or national affinity group. Agencies are beginning to lose personal lines customers to "group workplace marketing" programs offered at the individual's office or factory.

New competitors and new alternatives that circumvent agents (and their commissions) would be challenge enough for a P&C agency's management, but that's not all there is. Another societal and economic factor that has been every bit as damaging to P&C retailer's income flows is what might be called "the Wal-Mart factor." Thirty years ago, P&C agents handled the insurance for the neighborhood hardware store, druggist, garden shop, clothing stores, auto supply outlet, and dozens of others. Today, these retailers (their replacements, actually) are all under the same roof out in the suburbs, and they're all insured by their own captive insurance company. The local bank has been acquired by one of the big regionals. The once-loyal community hospital (remember those years you spent on their Board of Trustees?) is now part of some version of "NationsNet HMO PPO Conglomerate United." Even the local municipal entity is now subsumed under a county-wide "Uni-Gov" central political arrangement. The fact is that many of those old reliable commercial customers we used to depend on don't exist any more.

Likewise, retailer relationships with underwriting companies have been disrupted because the companies aren't configured in the same way (or don't exist) any more. There have been numerous major consolidations in the P&C underwriting business involving giant names like Aetna,

Home, and Continental. The survivors have new goals, new people, new business divisions with new products to sell, and have little appreciation for the ancient history of prior relationships with the predecessor's agents.

Consolidation has not ignored the retailing side either, as agencies and brokerages of every size have merged, acquired, or "clustered" together. Most people in the retail side of the business have lived through one or more versions of these activities; and if one has managed to avoid them, they certainly face competitors who have joined together. This trend has generated its own paradoxical counterpart — that of a new generation of start-up agency operations founded by former employees of larger shops who have determined they could do better on their own.

Life Industry Developments

Recently, life as a life insurance retailer has been just as chaotic, if not more so, than it has been on the P&C side. The problems besetting them resonate with those already discussed on the P&C side — demanding consumers, collapsing (or fickle) companies, increased regulation, problems attracting talented people, and brutal competitors.

Trust Betrayed

A recent spate of scandals involving the marketing practices of several big-name life insurance companies have generated a lot of negative publicity. More than a few life agents (one is tempted to call them "hucksters") have taken advantage of the elderly, the poor, and the ill-informed. Perfectly adequate policies were replaced with inadequate substitutes. Products were sold where none should have been. Overzealous marketing departments of life companies designed interest-sensitive products whose attractiveness was largely based upon the then higher prevailing interest rates in the 1980s. Such sales were based on unrealistic projections of policy cash-value growth; when such policies (especially so-called "vanishing premium" products) imploded for lack of internal growth, disgruntled consumers began looking for retribution. The populace, led often by class-action plaintiffs attorneys, rebelled against such practices. Insurance commissioners followed into the fray like crusaders. Agent misdeeds have been regularly tracked back to lack of appropriate levels of home-office supervision. In more serious cases, agents were found to have been actively encouraged in such practices by top-level company managers.

In recent years, competition in the life business rose to levels never before experienced. To maintain growth, or at least market share, many companies became lax and/or over optimistic in their underwriting and investment practices. Prices were set too low for the products they supported, risky investments fell apart, and the companies caught up in this turmoil fell into insolvency or rehabilitation. Hardly a company has gone unscathed. These episodes, continuing on the heels of the well-publicized problems of Executive Life, Fidelity Bankers, Mutual Benefit, Fidelity Mutual, Confederation Life, and a few other high-profile cases, have shaken the industry deeply, and have contributed to today's less than stable environment.

L&H "Brain Drain"

Due in part to the negative image arising from the problems mentioned above, the life retailing industry has found it increasingly difficult to attract talented new producers. LIMRA, the Life Insurance Marketing Research Association, reported that over the last 15 years the number of full-time career agents dropped by 23% (249,042 in 1981 to 192,750 in 1996). That rate has accelerated recently, with 19 percentage points of the drop coming in just the last five years of the study. Certainly (and thankfully), some of those departing people were required to leave, having participated in the scandals and bad practices that besmirched the industry.

Many of the agents recruited in the last twenty years were not properly trained, and could not (or sometimes would not) fully disclose the downside of the products they pitched. Many who were not aware of how their products would perform under less-optimistic scenarios were confused and ashamed when the low-interest '90s arose. Since many of these sales were to friends and family, these life people put as much distance as possible between themselves and the life industry — leaving in droves.

Increasing efficiencies brought about by shrinking margins are also contributing to the depletion of talent in the retail life sector. So, while the U.S. population grows, a greater proportion of the actual and potential insurance buying public here is being under-served or not served at all. According to LIMRA's 1996 Report (003572B-1296-24-OE46EXESUM), "Consumer Preferences Summary," 77% of those surveyed still expressed a preference for buying face-to-face, rather than by any other means. Similarly, more of those surveyed preferred buying from someone who represents an insurance company, over other alternatives such as a bank, credit union, or a stockbroker. However, while the insurance company representative was most preferred option, it was named by only 38%; leaving 62% of the life insurance-buying public available for a variety of alternative distribution systems to service.

Of special interest to the P&C industry (and readers of this book) was the strong preference voiced by survey participants for "multiple-line agents" who could offer auto and homeowners protection in addition to life insurance. The multi-line agent was preferred even over life agents who sold other financial products (e.g. mutual funds) although the younger the respondant, the greater the preference for offerings of "other" financial products.

The Shifting Product Mix

There's been a major shift in the makeup of premium income among most life insurance companies. According to the American Council of Life Insurance, from their *Life Insurance Fact Book*, the percentage of U.S. life insurance company premium receipts, representing "life insurance premiums" had steadily declined — from 43.8% in 1981 to 29.1% in 1990 (it has stayed relatively level since, developing 29.2% in 1995). Health insurance premiums have also dropped as a percentage of the total, from 30.1% in 1981 to 22% in 1990 (remaining fairly consistent, at 23.4% in 1995).

The big gainer among life company products has been in the sales of annuities, which grew from 26.1% in 1981 to 47.1% in 1995. This is significant for more than one reason.

With fewer premium dollars (as a percentage of the total) coming from life sales, the life industry is moving more toward an "assets under management" position. Life retailers have now become more direct competitors with other financial industry groups than they were when they marketed primarily "life" products. Instead of just competing with other life companies, life companies and retailers must now face off against stock brokers, banks, investment firms, and other financial giants.

The relative shift to annuities has direct implications for the commission-based retailer; the percentage of dollars handled that is paid to the retailer for annuities is much lower than for life products. "Working more for less" has become as much the demand for life retailers as it has for participants in every other industry in today's demanding, competitive, world economy.

New Distribution Alternatives

Increasingly, "simple" life products (usually in the term life category) are being marketed directly, through a number of channels. Direct television advertising, once restricted to the military-related or geriatric prospect, is now targeted to a much wider audience. Life "wholesalers" are using TV, radio, magazine, and Internet media to attract the comparison shopper of term life products.

Many banks are stepping up their life insurance marketing efforts, and recent bank-in-insurance deregulation will spur these efforts (see the next chapter on Strategic Planning for ideas relating to the insurance retailer finding opportunities in working with banks).

"Group workplace" or "worksite" marketing has been gaining in its share of the life dollar pie compared to other distribution methods. In the LIMRA study mentioned above, the workplace was second (behind the face-to-face sales process with an agent) as the public's preferred method of acquiring life insurance protection. Convenience, or ease of buying, seems to be the main benefit for consumers for this type of purchase. This points out that any retail insurance distribution system must not ignore the importance of ease of purchase for the potential customer. It's now obvious that we must build flexibility and no-hassle communication into any system we hope to profit from.

Revenue Pressures

As distribution systems become more efficient, competition increases, and mortality tables reflect a healthier, longer-lived populace, we can expect a continuation of downward pressure on life premium levels, particularly in the term insurance product group. Similar to the pressures on P&C retailers, L&H salespeople can expect these pressures to be compounded, for while premiums per unit of exposure can be expected to drop even more, at the same time competitive pressures will require that less of each (reduced) insurance dollar go to the distribution system.

Agents should expect to see a growing trend toward commission "levelization" in the life field, with inflated first-year commissions becoming more and more rare. As life products are required to compete on a "head to head" basis with other investment alternatives, and as modeling and comparison software systems become more transparent and easy to use, life products will be forced to allocate less of each dollar up front to the agent. The main reason is that it is the "earliest" dollars contributed to an investment that are most powerful in terms of compounding of growth — so it is the first dollars that must be allocated to the portfolio in greatest proportion.

Over the past decades, we have seen a continuing drop in the number of new individual lives being insured — especially in the "middle income" markets. In recent years, this trend has leveled off a bit and has been masked by the larger average face amount and higher average premium per policy (not per exposure unit) that are being sold today.

A Growing Need: To Redefine "The Insurance Agency"

There is no reason to think that the forces buffeting P&C and L&H retailers will diminish or disappear. Nor can we suppose that there will be no new competitive attacks on our dwindling customer base. It is much safer to assume that there will be an increasing barrage of these types of adversities. Clearly, an agency that continues to do things the way they were successfully done a few decades back is headed for decline (at least). A series of recurring challenges like these force those so assailed into deep introspection. We must ask, and answer anew, questions like "What is it that we really do?" "Who are we, anyway?" "What can we provide that the customer and the marketplace will continue to value?"

These questions, probed deeply enough, will cut right through the culture and established habits of our businesses. The answers rebounding from them should provide a map of sorts into the future. One of the great powers held by leaders is that of defining the world (at least provisionally), of explaining the situation to those involved in it. Agency leaders (or future leaders) asking these questions have an opportunity to create appropriate responses to the challenges we face. We have shown how attachment to the old definitions of an insurance retailer might well lead to its extinction. How, then, should we define our "world"? If we're not in the "insurance" business, what is it that we can do, that people today and tomorrow will pay us well to do? Traditional approaches to "insurance" are fast becoming as unable to support our livelihood as selling buggy whips became to our ancestors. What is it, at heart, that we do?

Insurance retailers sell business solutions. At first glance, this seems pretty simple — and not all that different from how we defined ourselves thirty years ago. Insurance, after all, is a response to a business problem. So why is this re-definition so critical? Let's go back to ABC Buggy Whip, Inc. (our fable, first mentioned in the Introduction).

Back to the Buggy Whip

It may have seemed only a semantic trifle for ABC to have re-considered themselves to be in the "transportation enhancement" business, instead of the buggy whip business. It was a "trifle" however, that meant the difference between survival and death. It was a "trifle" that recognized their heritage, their skills, their momentum, that did not radically undercut their values or their relationships, but that provided them a future (manufacturing seat covers, leather steering wheels, dashboard trim, etc.).

Just as people have always needed to travel from time to time, people and businesses have always needed security and economic stability. Since ancient times, the best hope for such security was to amass great quantities of wealth, preferably backed up by a well-outfitted garrison of soldiers. This option was available only to a lucky few. Others, at different times, may have been part of a close-knit community willing to pitch in with help when the home or barn burned down, or when a head of household was crippled by a charging bull. Insurance developed in response to these human needs. The need for security, stability and disaster recovery will continue as long as humanity does.

However, what insurance people actually deliver in the future will be as different from the mid-century agency models discussed in Chapter 1 as dashboards are from buggywhips. As we elaborate on what is encompassed by the proclamation that "We sell business solutions," in some ways the task may seem daunting. The changes will be culture-deep, and the scope of activity will be significantly expanded. We'll still be in the same business, however (as redefined), meeting the same basic human and economic needs, and we won't have to abandon our core values in the transformation.

Adding a Dimension

Insurance retailers' historical response to the human need for security and economic stability used to be pretty two-dimensional: "Buy insurance (a product), and we'll answer your questions about it (a service)." We will be recommending the addition of a third dimension: big-picture, customized help in the customer's overall strategic and business planning (i.e. customized consultation). After all, is traditional, two-dimensional insurance the only possible response to concerns about security and disaster recovery? We will argue that while these generic needs will remain constant, the way in which those needs will be met will continue to change, providing more options and flexibility in a way that will be faster, more efficient, and more cost effective.

Our increasingly sophisticated personal lines clients will have no problem with this re-definition of our agency; they will readily acknowledge that they are in the "business" of managing their households. Personal lines clients will be comfortable and open to the concept of the business of planning and protecting a family's future; and it is serious business indeed.

So what will we really have done by redefining our business? As we hope to show in the remainder of this book, doors can be opened to a world of broader opportunities. Building on what the insurance retailer already does (and knows how to do), we will encourage a subtle change, of direction and emphasis, that will lead to a future of promise and growth.

Chapter 3

Developing A Sales System and Nurturing A Selling Culture

The cross-selling of L&H products and cross-marketing of other services is successful to the extent that they are made a part of the sales organization's daily processes. Accordingly, a "dynamic sales organization" needs to be up and running, backed by the strategic vision and support of top management. As part of laying the foundation for such a sales organization, the ground must first be cleared of obstructions, such as those identified in Chapter 1. Consideration must be given to real changes in the retailer's psychological and cultural state, agency workflow designs, compensation and reward systems, company relationships, staffing, "political" issues, and other major concerns.

Jumping into a full-scale transition to cross-selling and cross-marketing would be too much all at once for a retailer whose systems weren't set up to support this expansion. By redesigning and "fine-tuning" the existing, P&C operation for better sales, while keeping in mind the transition to be made into expanded activities, these changes can be made in a fairly orderly manner. The goal is to redesign the agency today, with tomorrow in mind, and to implement the new designs so as to maintain continuity and profitability. This redesigned business will then be poised to accommodate the strategic planning issues that lead into cross-selling and cross-marketing.

Before You Expand — Are You Doing The P&C Part Right?

At the beginning of the "Computer Age," as businesses contemplated their automation options, savvy consultants would insist that they first get their manual systems in order. Why automate confusion and inefficiency?

Why speed up inaccuracy and sloppiness? If our files were in disarray, if we didn't consistently record and organize vital information, we were warned that computers would only speed up our business' self-destruction. Insurance retailers considering the new products, services, and marketing methods suggested in this book would do well to heed a similar caveat: take a good, hard look at your current systems and operations first. If a retailer is not performing exceptionally well in what should be its "core competency" (selling insurance), it would be unrealistic to expect success from trying to sell more products just as poorly.

"What does your agency sell?" While it is heard less often today than five years ago, we still hear P&C agents who answer this question with the platitude, "SERVICE!" Sorry, wrong answer. The better P&C agencies recognize that they sell "INSURANCE!" and they keep their attention and planning focused on this fact. Yes, service is a necessary component of the insurance product, but for well-organized agencies, service is a relatively minor *component* of what they sell — it is not what they sell. If you have any doubts, try this on a dozen or so of your best customers: send them an invoice for "Generic Service — no insurance included" (but don't plan your retirement on the proceeds).

There is an important distinction to be made in this context between "service" and "services" The former is an amorphous and misleading cliche´. "Services," however are very much a part of what progressive P&C agencies will be selling. We'll talk about many of them later on. For the time being, keep in mind that these "services" are "products," just like insurance policies are products. The central, defining word here is "*selling*."

Coming to this understanding has been a real breakthrough for many agencies. Once they seriously consider themselves to be primarily an "insurance sales organization," they have made the critical first step into the future. With this step, planning, activity, and everyday thinking begin to change and to be revitalized. A *sales* organization — it even sounds exciting!

There is another important step that is necessary to break through the constraints of thinking solely in terms of "P&C insurance sales." Before going there, let's take another good look at the insurance product itself, before we proceed to an examination of the makeup of a vital insurance sales organization.

Leveraging the Redefined Insurance Product

Fundamentally, insurance products are very simple, consisting of only two elements: a *financial transaction* plus an *information exchange system*. The financial transaction involves the payment of premiums in return for a promise to pay claims. With the accelerating proficiency and ubiquity of electronic funds transfers (EFT), we are seeing that computer and telecommunication networks are much better suited to moving money efficiently than are human hands. Similarly, on-line services, CD-ROM reference works, the Internet, "expert systems," knowledge databases, and similar outgrowths of the electronic age are all growing daily in their ability to answer questions and provide information when needed.

If computers and similar systems are so good at handling both basic elements of the insurance product, where then, is there opportunity for the insurance agent to add value to the product? Is the future of human beings in the insurance industry hopeless? Not yet. These automated tools force us to consider only specific, discreet parts of each element as logical points for human interface with the insurance system. If we do not find and cultivate these useful niches in the system wherein we can add value to the product, market forces will eliminate us from the transaction entirely. In fact, there are insurance distribution systems already in place and growing that "make do" almost entirely without the intermediation of agents or agencies. While these alternative distribution systems continue to expand in several areas, we believe that there still can be a viable role for insurance retailers to play well into the future.

First, in the "financial transaction" component, the retailer will continue to be well positioned for:

- selling the product in the first place - i.e., making the transaction happen;
- providing access to specific services, like customized loss control and safety advice, that will reduce the amount of claims, thereby lowering the consumer's premium (this adds value from the consumer's point of view, while maintaining profits and stability for the underwriter); and (in some cases)
- expediting the claims adjustment and payment process.

In the "information exchange system" component, the retailer will always be optimally positioned to:

- get accurate, reliable, and well-organized information to the underwriter;

- investigate the buyer's situation and particular problems, so as to suggest the best combination of insurance products and related services suited to the customer's needs; and (in some instances)
- be a source of, or provide a conduit for, answers to questions about the overall program, coverage features, and how the product "works."

Take a look at the job descriptions, duties, and individual tasks performed by each employee in your organization. If your business is paying people to perform anything other than the above-named functions (except necessary internal support functions like accounting), take another look. Then, find a way to quickly eliminate those jobs, duties, and tasks. Why? Because the marketplace will not continue to support non-essential activities that add no value for the consumer or the company.

Next, carefully review how your business undertakes those core competencies — these are the areas where your improvement efforts will lead to a competitive advantage. Since the first, and most important, component is the selling, focusing your efforts on sales process design and implementation will be most fruitful.

The Hallmarks of a Successful Insurance Sales Organization

Although it would be impossible to create a single set of criteria that fits all insurance retailers, there are certainly some common elements which contribute to success. Admittedly, the relative importance of some of these factors will depend upon the size and makeup of the agency. For example, the successful small agency run by a "relations-driven" unique personality, who focuses on a small number of large clients and develops all or most new business from referrals, will certainly look and operate quite differently than a large agency with a more typical hierarchy of principals, producers, and customer service reps. Similarly, a successful medium-sized agency with a mix of 90% of personal and 10% commercial lines will look and operate somewhat differently from an agency with similar revenues that are split 70% commercial and 30% personal lines. Even so, there are some characteristics and features of the successful insurance sales organization that are independent of these variables.

So what are these common, identifying characteristics of the successful sales organization that are "independent" of size, mix of business, and most other elements? In 1996, Conning & Company surveyed 85 "top-notch" independent agencies. They were asked: to identify their top 10 successful strategies. They responded (in order): target marketing, aggressive sales, cross-selling, carrier relations, customer relations, service, aggressive producers, reputation, automation, and telemarketing.[1]

In narrative form, this list might have the best agencies saying, "We work with our companies to identify products that will sell, use our automation and reputation to locate and attract prospects with the help of an ongoing telemarketing system, send out aggressive producers to sell those products, and we lock up customers with a great support system and active "total account selling" programs.

There are specialist and "boutique" agencies working with very narrow product lines that have developed unique programs that work for them, but careful analysis reveals that even these specialists have found a way to perform these tasks well. Most traditional P&C agencies that sell well have incorporated excellence in all the areas that are critical to sales success. Let's break it down in more detail by identifying the components that make up the type of dynamic sales organization that can guarantee growth and success.

Sales Culture "From the Top Down"

Top management in a successful agency (whether that means a sole proprietor or a group of owners/key executives), has a clear vision of who they are...and, just as importantly, who they aren't! Knowing that no business can be all things to all people, leaders of the best agencies keep a tight focus, so their shops never get bogged down in unattainable commitments, and don't get stretched so thin that the truly important things don't get done.

The leaders of such agencies are committed to sales effectiveness, they demand results and accept no excuses. That "nothing happens until a sale is made" is obvious to these people, and they insist that something happen! Consequently, they continually plan for, monitor, and encourage selling, throwing the bulk of the resources at their command behind the sales process.

Go into almost any of these agencies and you will experience a sense of energy — there's activity in the air. Producers aren't sitting around, wasting time; they're either on the phone with clients, or out on appointments. You'll notice a certain quiet competence among the CSRs and other staff, even if things appear to be pretty loose and casual, and you sense a quiet confidence — that there are effective controls in place and that these people really know what they're doing.

Strategic Planning and Active Follow-through

The best agencies develop a clear vision of who they are and where they're going by engaging in regular, serious, strategic planning. This process first involves "research and development" activities. In the smallest shops, this function involves reading, talking with peers, and staying in touch with the business community. Larger retailers may have one or more employees whose primary duty may be a more formal investigation into developing opportunities, impending changes, new products, and enhanced procedures for the agency to consider and perhaps implement. The very best organizations have this R&D function pervading the agency as a cultural value: everyone is responsible for "keeping up with the future." *Competing For The Future* by Gary Hamel and C.K. Prahalad and *Jumping the Curve* by Nicholas Imparato and Oren Harari are both outstanding inspirational books to get the creative juices flowing and to generate excitement for long-range planning.

Strategic plans are useless unless implemented, so real sales organizations translate their long-term strategies into action plans to be implemented, monitored, evaluated, and fine-tuned. With well-defined goals, these shops clearly demonstrate that they're living their strategy rather than just talking about it.

Quantifying and Benchmarking

In the best agencies each department, each employee, and every process is quantified and compared with industry benchmarks to identify weaknesses and strengths. Financial ratios are monitored and used for operational feedback. Specific employee and divisional goals (or personal goals for smaller retailers) are set, progress is tracked, and evaluations are communicated in relation to these goals. Goals are taken seriously, and excuses for non-performance are viewed negatively. We recommend *The Customer-Driven Company* by Richard C. Whiteley as an excellent sourcebook of techniques and procedures for measuring company performance.

The best agencies' employees are all aware of who the most valuable customers are, because measuring and internally communicating each customers' relative value to the organization is built into the system and widely communicated. Agency resources are consistently committed in proportion to a customer's value (and/or potential value) to the retailer.

Outstanding agencies view their database as a "gold mine," recognizing that they possess nothing more valuable than the information they have about their customers and prospects. They know that, second only to creating new sales, effectively managing their customer data and information is their most important activity. Even if the agency is not currently very effective at cross-selling L&H products and/or cross-marketing other services, there's an absolute commitment on the part of top management to become more effective at both, and know that the agency database is the springboard to these future plans.

Focusing on Individual Customer Needs and Developing Opportunities

Your clients' perceptions of what you're providing them in the way of goods and services and of how well you are doing the job, are different from what you think they are and, as the book *Selling The Invisible* by Harry Beckwith points out, they won't tell you. Just as the strongest individuals thrive on constructive criticism and direction, the best sales organizations constantly solicit feedback and suggestions from their customers. This process should be handled in such a manner as to encourage frank comments and criticism — one of the best methods is to outsource this function to a third party, who canvasses a sample by telephone on a regular basis. People are more comfortable criticizing others on the phone than face-to-face or in writing, and they are more forthcoming when the suggestions can be given to someone other than the party being reviewed.

Similarly, a strong sales organization should have built-in, reliable, and consistent procedures for receiving, handling, and expediting the resolution of complaints. Employees must immediately document all complaints, and such documentation should reliably trigger a series of events that will guarantee both a solution to the problem and a formal investigation into the cause.

Both formal customer feedback and complaint handling systems are really just subsets of the larger responsibility taken very seriously by cutting-edge sales organizations — that of promoting and maintaining a constructive dialogue with each customer. This dialogue is managed with the specific objectives of first determining and then keeping pace with the needs of that individual customer, so that the products and services offered for sale are of true value. The goal of this dialogue management is the building of long-term, profitable relationships with customers who would find it expensive and painful to move their business to a competitor.

Automating Efficiently

There's no way around it: for the foreseeable future, insurance retailers must plan to spend from 3% to 5% of annual revenues every year to acquire and maintain the automation tools required for them to compete and grow profitably. This is as true of the two-person shop with $200,000 of revenues as it is of the largest national brokers. Obviously, the larger an organization is, the easier it is to allocate a greater percentage of resources to automation and if these investments are well-planned, they will lead to even further growth and advantage over the competition.

Automation, of course, doesn't just mean computers. Agency automation strategies should encompass telephony, fax, printing, e-mail, cellular, and other technologies. These systems should be acquired and integrated to make it easier to do more of the agency's core activities, more efficiently. Every purchase and addition should be considered in the light of what it will add to the ability to sell products and services and/or communicate with customers, vendors, and strategic partners.

The successful agency today, whether small or large, understands the power of technology. Actually, technology today and tomorrow will offer as many, if not more, advantages to the small and medium-sized agency as it will to the large agency. The well-equipped small agency will be increasingly able to look and act like the "big guys." For the larger organizations, some of the operating efficiencies and productivity increases which technology has been promising, but not yet really delivering on, will finally begin to materialize, allowing them to truly benefit from the enhanced computer power they will be able to afford (see more on the power of technology in chapter 7).

Managing Relationships With Vendors

There's no point in selling if there is nothing to sell. Insurance retailers, by definition, sell something "made" by someone else (usually an underwriting company). As a result, they require access to the source of these products. This access is gained and optimized through the intelligent management of agency relationships with their companies. We all know of agencies who seem to get better pricing and more flexible terms from their carriers than others can. These differences often translate into making a sale where none otherwise would have occurred. The most successful agencies take this business task very seriously indeed, and commit significant time and resources to ensuring that they are viewed by their vendors as "best in class."

These preferred relationships are not maintained simply by "schmoozing." Equally as important, over time, are the smallest details of every contact between agency and company — each account-current payment, each phone call, and every field underwriter's visit. Something as obvious as a commercial lines submission speaks volumes about how much an agency values its relationship with the underwriter: is it complete, neat, honest, well-organized, presenting the "big picture," and submitted so as to provide a real possibility for the business to actually be written? If so, and if done so consistently, that agency will find that it can get a lot more done than can the somewhat slipshod outfit over in the next town.

These relationships certainly don't need to be managed as one-way, either. One mid-sized agency has a formal procedure for advising each one of its vendors (insurance companies, wholesalers, and service providers) how many "stars" they earned in the agency's evaluation of the prior year's performance. The agency's president explains each year, to the vendor's top regional management, that one "star" can be awarded to the agency's vendors in the following five categories:

1. Significant (top ten in size) in revenues for the agency
2. Fast growing (double-digit percentage over the prior year)
3. Provide exclusive or semi-exclusive access to significant, competitive products
4. Pay above-average commissions, or provide above-average revenue opportunities, in the lines or services provided
5. Provide above-average profit-sharing, bonuses, or override opportunities on the products vended

An additional, sixth item is available to either add or subtract from the total above, for "intangibles" — fun to work with, reliable, loyal, etc.

This "star" ranking is then used, not only to express appreciation and communicate a strategic commitment, but also to communicate areas in which the company could improve, from the retailer's standpoint.

Coordinated Marketing, Advertising, and Public Relations Programs

The term "marketing," as used here, means the presentation of a company and its products to the consuming public, rather than the "placement" functions undertaken to submit business to underwriters. The best agencies are sophisticated marketers, and carry out coordinated marketing programs. Such programs incorporate integrated approaches to market research, prospecting, contact automation, advertising, community and public relations, sales calls, and follow-up functions.

Considerable thought is given to "image" details, which include letterhead, Internet web pages, office signage, business cards, proposals, brochures, and advertisements in various media. A consistent message and identity is presented, one that builds awareness and confidence among prospects and customers. Once or twice a decade all retailers should revisit their "image" strategy with the assistance of competent, creative design professionals. This is to make sure that the agency's "message" is still timely and coherent, and effectively delivers the quality and competence message desired.

The top-flight agency is "visible" in the community, whether the scope of that community is local, regional, or national. Their leaders understand that though the organization might be of top quality, if nobody knows about it, the quality is of little consequence. A reputation without repute is of little value. Successful sales organizations know how and when to promote themselves both internally to existing clients and prospects, as well as externally to the general public, to key legal, accounting, and banking advisors. When their name is mentioned, people often say, "Yes, I've heard very good things about that firm."

Professional Sales Management

Insurance retailers can be "pretty good" at all the other activities listed in this section and still succeed marvelously if they are "great" at sales management. In the smallest shops, the entrepreneurial-minded owner manages his or her own sales activity, and rarely lets up on the self-imposed pressure. As agencies have grown, many have lost sight of this absolutely critical function at one or more stages of their development and have plateaued or declined in size as a result. In recent decades, some have found it easier to achieve "growth" by acquiring other retailers, but for many this has just made their problems bigger rather than solving them.

Unless and until sales management functions are revived and maintained, the agency is wasting its resources and squandering its heritage.

Here is another area where many agencies will need outside help. Any number of good consultants are available to move the process along. The authors have had recent contact with Dick Womack, Joan Sansing, and others and have included some suggestions from each one in this and later sections of the book. We encourage agencies to investigate these, and other sources you can uncover on your own, and give serious consideration to letting a couple of outsiders "tear your operation apart" every five years or so. We can almost guarantee, though that a unfailing recommendation from any of them will be to constantly improve sales management skills and to manage sales aggressively.

Professional sales management requires, at the minimum, the following:

A Professional Sales Manager

In growing from a small to a medium-sized agency, many an entrepreneur has learned they have no head for business management. Many others find that, while they can both "produce" and run the place, both jobs suffer for their trying to do both. A very different skill set is required for the two jobs. It is the same with sales management. Similarly, it is unusual indeed for a great sales person to have the aptitude or personality required for sales management. Salespeople need managing, and this points to the obvious corollary: they aren't managers!

When the number of producers at a retailer grows much beyond a half-dozen or so, it is time for the owners to search for, recruit, and acquire a professional sales manager. If every producer isn't producing, if agency revenues aren't growing, if excuses are heard more than shouts of triumph, it definitely is time. Such people can be found already managing successful sales programs in other industries — the products sold are far less important than the career success of the sales manager. One of the best sources is the ranks of the life industry — regional and district managers of the major life companies get tired of endless transfers, and have often gone as far as they might with their company. Many are ready for a change — just ask them! Then hold them accountable, and get out of the way!

Goal Setting and Reviews

Each agency, each of its departments, and every salesperson in them must regularly set, in consultation with the sales manager, clearly-defined, quantified sales goals. These are set in the context of the experience, specialties, market conditions, opportunities, and company relationships that exist. Such goals are then subdivided both by time period and by individual tasks (number of calls to be made, prospects identified, referrals to be obtained, accounts to be rounded, closings to be finalized, etc.). Then, activity is reported, monitored for accuracy, and then firm feedback is given for any numbers not meeting the target goal.

No Tolerance for Excuses

"Firm feedback" includes everything up to, and including, termination. When a retailer has incorporated every other element of a real sales system as outlined here, real salespeople will produce — with no excuses. The fact is some people can't sell. Some of those who can sell, don't, or won't for whatever reason. Some who used to sell, sell no more. Get rid of them, or at least transfer them to a non-selling job, so that no one in the organization is confused and doubt the owners' resolve.

Nothing will sabotage a retailer's sales efforts more surely than a producer who is kept on "because he's not costing us any money." Wrong, wrong, wrong! Nobody will believe you are serious about selling if *you* aren't serious about selling! To push the analogy implied in the phrase sales culture," one single smidgen of non-selling "mold" will infect and poison the entire batch of developing penicillin. You know who they are — they haven't sold a significant account in months. Give them a warning, give them a minimum goal, and if they fall short, give them "the boot."

Regular Sales Meetings

The sales manager will get the crew together periodically, so that successes may be acknowledged, failures talked over, and team spirit fostered. At some meetings, a bit of technical knowledge might be shared, or a new product introduced. From time to time, bring in an underwriter who is important to your goals. Once every other month seems to work for some agencies, particularly those with multiple offices. Others meet every week at a given time. In addition to these scheduled meetings, when the sales process is really humming along, producers will gather spontaneously to brainstorm, problem-solve, and plan a team approach to major prospects.

Sales Skills Training

Few people graduate from high school knowing how to sell effectively. Even those rare individuals who are sales "naturals" should be expected to get even better as they gain experience. Most sales managers have been to the seminars, taken the training, read the literature, and have learned from the best. They in turn require that the producers in their charge do the same. "How to Sell" is beyond the scope of this book, but learning how to sell better should be one of the career goals of all who read it.

Good sales managers often accompany their charges on sales calls; better sales managers will accompany their journeyman producers silently, letting them grope their own way, leading them only later, post-call conversation, to point out what was strong, and what could have been done better.

Lead Generation and Maintenance

Good sales organizations constantly generate leads, in a variety of ways, through a tightly-managed, well-planned program. Leads are transformed into "suspects," suspects into "prospects," which are in turn converted to "customers." The section below on "sales center" activities goes in to some of the details of setting up and maintaining such a program.

Product and Activity "Focus" Management

"Any seasoned sales manager will confirm that producer "activity" is necessary, but not sufficient, for sales success. Making forty phone calls in a day is hard work, as is knocking on a couple of dozen doors. Still, we all have known well-intentioned aspirants who called all one day, and knocked all the next, and wound up the week with no new customers. Having the right people on the production team selling the right products to the right prospects is much more effective. Sales must be effectively managed in this dimension as well.

Because each retailer is located in a certain region, and represents certain markets, and has experience with certain industries, they can be more successful leveraging those certain advantages. The more productive retailers have developed "niches" that they exploit, whether these be in certain industry groups (construction or not-for-profits, for instance), or in certain product lines used as "door openers" (D&O, perhaps, or workers compensation).

Sales managers must always maintain awareness and control over producer activity — to be sure they are working their strengths and not getting lost in random "busy-ness." Producers that are "on goal" and proven should be allowed a certain latitude to try working in new areas with some of their time — but this "freestyling" should never take up the majority of anyone's time. Such efforts are most successful when they are directed at specific prospects, and when the attempt is to build a relationship of confidence, over time, through regular and persistent efforts.

Activities are further monitored and directed in the better shops with the assistance of automated systems for tracking, developing, and acquiring prospects, turning them into customers with systematic campaigns of calls, letters, brochures, visits, and proposals. In chapter seven we will go into the uses and choices for such systems under the heading "Sales Force Automation."

Sales Team Coordination

The days of the Lone Ranger are long gone. When it comes to larger commercial accounts, an agency should be sending out well-coordinated ad-hoc teams, consciously put together to match agency skills, experience, and personalities with the prospect's people, needs, and industry. The sales manager needs to oversee and direct these team efforts.

Compensation and Motivation Systems That Work For, Not Against, Profit

As pointed out above, there is no hesitation, among the leaders of the best agencies to fire consistently unproductive producers, and to fire them quickly. At the same time, in such agencies, compensation arrangements are designed to actually reward results that lead to the agency's success. As the business environment and our industry have changed and evolved, the need has grown to scrutinize old truisms, to question "the way we've always done things" — those ways may be inappropriate or counterproductive today.

This point returns us to the underlying theme: cross-selling and cross-marketing. Why should we sell more products and services to the customers we already have. The reason is competitive advantage and the profits that arise from it. The selling cycle proposed here is to learn about the customer, use that knowledge to recognize or anticipate needs, and then provide access to solutions that meet those needs. In this way, we are useful to the customer, who trusts us with more information and concerns and expends energy to teach us about his or her preferences and goals. This added knowledge again is turned to recognizing problems and solving them for the customer through the provision of more products and services.

Loyalty and a sustainable competitive advantage is developed in this way. It would require considerable effort for your customer to teach a competitor everything that your organization already has learned about the customer's situation and preferences. This process generates the only *sustainable* competitive advantage — your intimate knowledge of your customer (price, product features, and service level can all be duplicated by your competitors).

While this competitive advantage is being developed, revenues for your organization are being generated. These revenues arise, not from expensive, time-consuming, hit-or-miss new sales efforts, but from customers that your people are already calling on and comfortable with. Voila! More revenue per sales call! More revenue per customer! More profits!

Do our compensation systems recognize this new order of business? Not at all. Rare is the P&C (or L&H) operation whose pay plan is in alignment with or recognizes the true value of individual customers. Retailers wishing to grow have come up with the same, knee-jerk method for obtaining growth, which has been to pay a bonus for new customers. Never mind that new customers are the most expensive to obtain; forget that new customers have a higher attrition rate than established ones. The upshot of this thinking has been that most compensation plans are designed to reward *activity*, rather than *results*. If, as is almost always the case, long-time customers are of more strategic value to the retailer than new ones, compensation arrangements should reflect this.

In addition to salespeople, all other employees should also be compensated in some way relative to the real growth and profitability of the retailer. CSAs and CSRs, receptionists, accounting staff, computer network technicians — the work of every one of these touches directly or supports the pleasing of the customer and the underwriter (if not, they have no business being paid at all). To some degree every staff person should feel, in their pocketbook, the rises and falls of the employer's fortunes.

Earlier, the necessity of team selling of major accounts was presented. At this turn, an appendant requirement appears — that no producer be permitted to imagine they "own" any account. Cross-selling and cross-marketing (indeed, even the step-by-step development of prospects into customers) require that every person in the organization have immediate access to every pertinent fact about a customer, so that when the customer calls, or writes, or visits, the responding person (whomever that may be) at the agency is "up to speed" and knows what is going on. Agency operations must be designed so that a close relationship with every customer endures, whether any individual employee dies, retires, is fired, or gets drafted by the NBA. The agency "has" customers; the employee "has" a job; if by doing that job well the employee ensures the customer stays your agency's customer, the employee should be rewarded. In the event any proprietary notions arise between producers as to an account, jump in to cut them off — in the long run, the customer will not be as well served when such notions prevail.

Accordingly, we recommend that each employee's performance relative to increasing the agency's value be reviewed for year "one," and that compensation for year "two" be based upon that prior year's success, with opportunities, in some positions at least, to earn further bonuses for outstanding work in year "two." Forget about paying a percentage of commission — that only reinforces deluded ideas of account ownership. You may well "back in" to the salary by considering the commissions that have arisen from a producer's work, but keep the math to yourself. Sales at a high level is extremely hard work, and requires rare talent and considerable experience. Reward successful sales efforts handsomely, in such a way as to make clear that the paycheck is the producer's, but the customer is not.

Just because existing, long-term customers are of more value to the retailer than are new customers, this does not imply that new customers should not be cultivated. On the contrary, new accounts are vitally important to any agency. Old accounts, valuable as they might be, go bankrupt, are acquired, move away, die, or are snagged by competitors despite our best efforts and intentions. Without new business, agencies would eventually fade to the point of extinction. So, there should be incentives to employees for bringing in new customers. We suggest, though, that there be less of a bonus available for the first policy or service sold to a new customer than for the third, or the fifth line of coverage or service provided subsequently. Every attention should be given to developing new, monoline customers into full-fledged, loyal, and dependent business relationships as quickly as possible.

The Constant Battle Against the "Diminishing Returns Paradox"

One of the oddest things about the retail P&C industry is that the our best producers run out of time first. Think about it — every account sold requires attention, and some of that attention is expected (by the customer) to come from the producer or production team that first sold it. For example, many agents and brokers have their producers "market" their own accounts — presenting them to underwriters, explaining and answering questions, negotiating pricing and terms. There are obvious advantages to this system, but it also means that producer who brings in the most business to be marketed runs out of selling time first.

The top management of the best retailers recognize this paradox, hate it, and actively battle against it with determination. They know how rare and precious is the warm body that can sell a big account, and they design agency workflows and operations in such a way as to have those few, rare people who can sell, actually selling almost all the time. Every other task that might distract these "rainmakers" from making their appointed rounds is delegated, transferred, intercepted, or handled by someone competent to the task and familiar with the account, but unable to sell well.

Yes, much of this sales activity can and should be calls on existing customers, seeking ways to help these customers even more. But, answering the phone, returning voice-mail, writing letters, straightening out a claim, or anything else that *can* be done by anyone else, *should* be done by someone else. Agencies that don't have the back-office brainpower to handle these ancillary functions need to hire and/or develop it, and expect to pay for it. If, by bringing in five $60,000 super-CSAs to support your best producer, that producer could grow his or her contribution to the agency's book from $400,000 to $1,400,000, would your organization be ahead? The answer is obvious.

"But we don't pay CSAs fifty or sixty thousand dollars! That would upset our entire compensation system." Of course it will. Upset is right, and long overdue. Your organization won't change from a staid, mid-century "like Granddad did it" shop into a dynamic selling machine without big changes, painful upsets, and smashed idols.

Networking with Other Sales and Marketing Professionals

In a rapidly-changing world, no one organization can keep up internally with every development that might affect it. In this "networked age" we all truly need to be networking — with our peers, our companies, our customers, and others. In the best agencies, almost every employee keeps their eyes and ears open for developments that might affect business, and this awareness is encouraged, recognized, and rewarded.

Many organizations exist to foster this networking activity. The "Big I" (Independent Insurance Agents) and Professional Insurance Agents (PIA) organizations foster communication at the local, state, and national levels. Agency "clusters" have flourished for the benefit of the smaller shops. Several franchise organizations have tested the waters of insurance retailing, including the ISU franchise (most active now in the Western states). Membership affiliations of independent agencies include "Group 500," Assurex, and Associated Risk Managers International — each have hundreds of agency members and are growing in importance and geographic spread.

Find a vital, growing insurance retailer of almost any size and you will find a member of at least one, and often two or three, of these types of industry organizations. Even the largest national brokers, with their massive resources and research departments, share certain resources and systems with one another, for their mutual benefit.

Development of Strategic Partners

Great insurance retailers don't just have their people out on the street wearing out shoe leather. Such efforts only augment the greater stream of business, which arises from the spring of strategic alliances. The better part of sales success comes after trust and confidence is established, and these come quickest when a solid introduction leads the way. Such introductions are made through special arrangement with a few key collaborators.

To start with a very straightforward example, and one close to the heart of this book, consider the L&H agency down the street or across town. Because of their long cultivation of trust with their clients, the leaders of these agencies are often asked to help in other insurance matters. Some have picked up a P&C contract or two, perhaps have brought in a producer to help with this side of things. Such arrangements, though, meet only some of the needs they are called upon to provide. When L&H agents handle P&C as a hobby or an afterthought, they get little more from such efforts than do P&C retailers who write a life policy from time to time.

Why not confer with one another, and introduce each other to clients that have need of the other's resources? The "sales" that arise from such beginnings require comparatively little selling; they come about in fact rather automatically.

The same sort of arrangement may be made with business consultants, accountants, attorneys, human resources firms — in fact with almost any kind of business that is already providing valued services to customers you'd love to insure. Such relationships can take time to develop, and there has to be more than just the perception that there is value for both parties for them to continue. Insurance sales consultant Mona Carpenter suggests that agencies take the first step, bringing business to the prospective partner, rather than asking for some business from them.

Perhaps you have a long-standing relationship with a mid-sized manufacturer that vends its products through a multi-state dealer network. Your client wants to cinch up the ties that connect them to these dealers, and what better way to do this than by providing them access to valuable, money-saving services. A golden opportunity exists for the perceptive agency — set up a special insurance program for these dealers, save them money, and get access to them for all types of needs.

Very few businesses exist today that don't belong to one or more associations. While "association business" has been ridden so hard as to become a cliche´, many opportunities still exist there. Ask your client who the top officers are in their state or national association. Then ask for an introduction (again, thanks to Mona Carpenter for this tactic) — they'll be glad to provide it. Just take the ball and run!

Recruiting, Training and Mentoring Coordinated with Perpetuation Plans

To attract energetic, talented, intelligent people, a sales organization must first demonstrate that the system is in place that will support them as salespeople — in the manner to which they hope soon to become accustomed. If all the other critical issues outlined here are implemented, this system will be in place, and the booming retailer will have people knocking on their door, hat in hand, asking for the chance to work there. How to chose among them? We've heard of no better formula than that put forth by Dick Womack, who led McGriff, Siebels, and Williams from deep-south obscurity to national prominence as a P&C broker.

Mr. Womack says that a prospective employee will not, repeat, *will not*, ever be a great producer unless they possess, before hiring, what he calls “the Five E’s”:

- *Ego.* A strong sense of self, a self-confidence that projects itself as something that approaches the quality of charisma. Every great producer believes deeply that they are great, as human beings, and they carry themselves with an attitude that shows this.

- *Empathy.* “These people have so much ego, in fact,” Mr. Womack insists, “the only thing that keeps them from eating their own young is the quality of empathy.” To succeed in sales, one must be able to recognize and feel the troubles of the customer in one’s own heart — this empathy causes great producers to want to help their business clients.

- *Economic Drive.* Great producers want money, and the things that money will bring. The more money they want, the more they will sell (as long as compensation is tied, in some manner, to the results they produce for their employer). How rich does your prospective producer seem to want to become?

- *Energy.* Great producers bounce out of bed in the morning and sprint through the day, working late into the night when need be. And then they spring out of bed again the next morning. We all know empathetic people with big egos that would like to be rich, but just don’t have the gumption to crank out the work that is required. No energy, no sales.

- *Ethics.* Mr. Womack warns that “Nothing will destroy your agency quicker than a producer who plays fast and easy with the truth and with your reputation.” If you can spot them coming in the door, give them “the boot.” Once hired, let them all know where you stand. At the first transgression of truth and honor, fire them. Period.

Really talented employees will stay with you only if they acquire a “piece of the action.” Don’t give it away, but do sell it, at favorable terms to them. Many an agency owner has reached retirement age with no one to turn to for cashing out other than a spendthrift son and a penurious backup producer. Such situations often result in "fire sale" situations that reward the owner precious little for a lifetime of labor. Hire good people, pay them well, and as soon as they prove themselves, start "selling" the business to them.

Given the ease, accuracy, and availability of psychological testing for insurance recruits, it would be silly to ever hire someone without going through this step. We know of agencies who test all applicants, but still hire in contravention to the results of the test. They get what they deserve. At the very least, if results indicate doubtful performance, get another test or two. If the answers are unanimously cautioning, take heed. If one or more tests are favorable, proceed with care — there are more than a few applicants out there who can think their way around all but the most complex testing procedures — these are the same people who could hurt you the most.

Training and Mentoring

New producers have much to learn. Better retailers have a formal program that imparts knowledge in both insurance and sales in a planned, systematic fashion. Whether your shop utilizes full-blown training programs or develops and runs them in-house, this is a step that must not be overlooked.

Rare indeed is the commercial P&C producer that can bring in significant revenue in their first year. Rather, use this training-intensive period as a time for mentoring, during which the novice trails along with a carefully-selected senior producer, learning the ropes as they go. This relationship can be mutually beneficial, as the senior party is re-ignited by youth and enthusiasm, and dares not fail, since his or her every step is being watched. The younger party, in turn, learns by doing, helping out with various tasks and duties required to put together and maintain a sales relationship with a customer. The trainee is weaned from this direct relationship with the mentor by incorporating her or him into various ad hoc sales team efforts by the beginning of that producer's second year.

Before the first six months has passed, though, the agency's sales manager and the mentor will know if they are working with gold or gloss. If there is little hope for real success with the person, do everyone a favor and let him or her go. If the person is "right," their eyes will light up and they will pounce on opportunities to sell something, to sell anything. They will be quick to understand that sales arise from needs, which can be uncovered through skillful questioning. Don't let your weak producers mislead you — any experienced sales manager will tell you that a failing producer will blame the training program, while a truly talented trainee will insist that the training program get out of their way.

The initial year of employment in our complex and evolving business is, of course, just the beginning of training. At better agencies, the entire staff is well-trained and getting better. Learning and professional growth are major facets in the corporate culture. Almost everyone in the agency is enrolled in some kind of course or designation program; "continuing education" is not a requirement, it is a way of life.

"Sales Center" Activities

Suppose your P&C agency has all the critical components of a sales organization discussed above — management, motivation, personnel, products, automation, brochures, etc. You could still be "dead in the water" if your people are sitting around with plenty to sell and no one to sell to. Insurance sales require appointments; more good appointments guarantees more sales. Often handled as an afterthought, even in some mid-size and larger agencies, the generation of a steady stream of good appointments is an absolutely essential element for the survival of today's agency.

A "sales center" is comprised of those activities of an agency (whether done internally or outsourced), whereby leads are generated and appointments and other sales campaign processes are scheduled.

New Producers and Prospecting

One of the authors' partners likens the provision of leads to a producer to "salting the birds' tails" — asserting that anyone could have some success in selling to an unending string of provided, qualified appointment leads. We agree; in fact, we think that requiring a trainee producer to generate a significant number of appointments for themselves and their mentor serves at least three important functions. First, this is a very reliable screen for a new hire — it confirms if they have the energy to call, ask, struggle and try. Working to get appointments also reveals just how much stomach a producer has for rejection and "failure." The new producer's sales manager and mentor can also discern whether any "sales sense" is present — does the trainee understand that you have to ask, and ask, and ask again in a variety of ways to generate a significant number of sales?

Second, the producer trainee gains an understanding of and appreciation for the difficulty and costs involved in securing appointments, by personally experiencing the multiple telephone calls, the mailings, and the personal visits required to land an account. A producer who has this ingrained sensitivity will be less likely to squander a lead or appointment that might be provided to him or her later in their career. If a producer works only half her ex-dates, or only seriously prepares for half his appointments, each ex-date and every appointment instantly costs the agency twice as much! Similarly, hardened producers will be more likely to "jump" on any opportunity or potential lead they might run in to in the normal course of going about their lives — recognizing these chances for the rare and precious commodities they really are.

Finally, having new producers work a good bit at generating their own appointments makes good economic sense for the agency. As we will see below, obtaining "ex dates" and appointments is somewhat costly, but not expensive when compared with the value of a successful producer's selling time. In most producers' first couple of years, that producer costs their employer money — usually generating short-term losses rather than profits. Why not offset some of those costs by having trainees do something that you'd have to pay someone else to do if they weren't such as working the phone and sending out letters?

This means that part of the producer's initial training includes telephone prospecting techniques and a thorough introduction to the agency's marketing philosophy and marketing system components. Role playing, practice, and "over the shoulder" criticism and encouragement all play a part early in this process. Also, the agency's sales management, marketing department and mentor have to meticulously oversee the selection of who the trainee is calling. Start them out with a good list of "suspects" for a competitive product that your agency has easy access to. Pointing them to *The Yellow Pages* is definitely not enough.

Persistency must be managed as well — it is the rare account that is sold in a simple, direct sequence — the first call resulting in a pleasant appointment, an easy application, a friendly presentation, and a quick closing. Producers must be required to recognize and act on the "value of the database." It costs the agency money, time and resources to find out even a little about a given prospect. That "little" can be incrementally grown, through a number of contacts, into a "lot" of useful information over time. If handled pleasantly and professionally, each subsequent contact with a prospect and every single request for more information actually forms a part of the relationship required to complete a sale. Remember: information gathering is not an impediment to what we really want to do (i.e. sell); rather, it is one of the very few ways in which the agent adds value to the insurance product — it is what we are paid to do!

Even if the prospecting activity reveals there is no "fit" at this time between the agency's products and the prospect's needs, all information gathered needs to be treated with respect. Just as the agency's product lines constantly change; the problems and needs of a prospect change as well. Only by staying in touch will your organization be poised to respond with "the solution" at the time your prospect becomes aware of the problem, but without the data from prior contacts being readily available, every such opportunity will have to start all over again from the ground floor. If, by chance, the prospect should remember you or your agency, they will likely resent having to answer all the same questions a second or third time for you. If you can't remember what they told you, how can you be trusted to protect their business?

Seasoned Producers and Prospecting

A well-organized telemarketing campaign can generate good commercial "ex dates," in quantity, for around $15 to $20 apiece. A sizable list of such ex-dates can then be worked into sales appointments for additional costs ranging from $100 to $200 per appointment. These costs include wages for experienced, well-managed telemarketing and direct marketing specialists. The "shop rate" for such specialists might run from $30 to $50 per hour — including business overhead and profits to be expected from the work. The telemarketer's wages are about half this amount.

The rarest and most costly resource of any P&C agency is their experienced producers' time. At some point in the transition from "trainee" to "experienced producer," an individual's time is too precious to use in mass prospecting and bulk marketing. We suggest that each agency study their activity and costs enough to approximate the net revenues from real sales activities. Whether your agency earns $200 or $400 or $600 an hour when your producers are actually selling face to face, it makes little sense for experienced, competent salespeople to be on the telephone trying to get appointments — a function that can be handled adequately by much lower-cost people.

The "prospecting" of mid-level and senior producers should be limited, for the most part, to gaining referrals from, and networking with, existing qualified prospects and clients. Producers also contribute by providing detailed descriptions of just what kinds of prospects they work with best, and by generating feedback on the quality of leads and appointments they have been given. Apart from these functions, agency management must recognize its responsibility to its best producers, that of keeping the "appointment pipeline" of these precious people full.

Gathering information, marketing, and selling — it's what we're paid to do. While our P&C agency model indicates that selling cannot be delegated (it should be our "core competency"), we do need to take a closer look at "ex dating" and appointment setting. These latter two functions are critical components of the sales process for insurance and related products. Therefore, they must be handled professionally, by experts. This does not necessarily mean, though, that they must be handled "in-house." The alternatives: develop an professional "in-house" direct marketing team, or "outsource" the task to professionals.

Maybe you've told yourself, "I'm not going to support any telemarketing function for my agency — I hate telemarketers! I hang up on them every day at home! Why should we do direct mailings? Everybody throws that junk away." Maybe you're wrong. Telemarketing today supports more than 5 million jobs, is used by more than 500,000 companies, and is directly involved in over $280 billion in annual sales of goods and services in the United States alone.

Ten years ago there were approximately 50 firms that provided telemarketing assistance oursourced from other companies; that number is over 1000 today. For every insurance organization that had a direct marketing program in 1987, ten do so now (these figures provided by Larry Neilson, President of NMS - see Appendix 2). Even though your P&C agency may not be aware of this growth, your competitors are — and are likely putting it to good use. Very simply, a well-designed and professionally managed direct prospecting system gets your salespeople where they can do the most good — in front of prospects who are interested in your story.

ENDNOTE

1. Victoria Sonshine Pasher, "Agency Ranks To Fall 19% by 2006" *National Underwriter*, Property & Casualty edition, February 3, 1997, p. 43.

Chapter 4

Selecting and Implementing an Expanded Sales Strategy

Sometimes we learn from our failures, from examining our weaknesses, or from stating things in the negative. Those same 85 top-notch agencies surveyed on their perceived "strengths" by Conning & Company also admitted their top ten weaknesses. They included: producer recruitment/training, lack of new sales, automation, poor management, unmotivated staff, agent/carrier interface, no staff training, inadequate revenue, poor marketing, and poor quality CSRs.

Thus, even the better agencies acknowledge that they could be a lot more profitable (and their companies would be a lot happier) if they got a handle on attracting, training, managing, and motivating their staff to use automation and marketing systems to bring in the big sales numbers.

To achieve these goals, strategic planning is required. In planning an addition to an existing building, the architect pays close attention to the original building, to the features of the site as a whole, and to intended use of the new wing. Similarly, early in the planning process for expansion of an ongoing agency, it is critical to take stock of the current situation, the present and anticipated future environment, and to gain clarity about the direction in which the principals wish it to grow. Resources for growth are finite, however, there are many possible paths to "growth" and finding close-to-optimal solutions to the growth problem is perhaps the major challenge facing agency leadership today.

A "strategic plan" shouldn't be some obscure document gathering dust on a shelf. Rather, your plan should be a living, adaptable set of carefully thought-out plans and contingencies, regularly evaluated and altered to fit the changing times. Such a plan should include "action plans," and if a few of these don't copy any of the past models of doing business, your firm's chances of survival are greater. However, exploring "unknown territory" is not for the fainthearted; frequently serious analysis never gets completed at some agencies because no one has the courage to carry it through a conclusion that could force real change. Many of those who do start the planning process take the easy way out, deciding that what they have been doing is probably good enough, and then work the analysis backwards in order to justify the status quo.

There also needs to be a certain amount of "R&D" in any organization for long-term survival. Of course, not all new projects and plans prove successful, but there is still a benefit to having tried something new. Taking a fairly conservative approach in terms of the financial resources that are committed, have your people dive in wholeheartedly to small-scale experiments. So long as you have the sense to recognize when one tactic is not working, when another is showing real potential, and take the appropriate action, there is the promise of success. In the future, if you're not trying fresh approaches regularly, learning from your mistakes and capitalizing on your successes, you're going to be left out of the game.

Agency Self-Analysis

Agency principals who have determined that growth is a necessary element of their future success must then face the question: Grow how? The first step to finding an optimal set of answers to this question is to gain a clear understanding of the current "state of the agency." Honest, inquisitive, introspective people have learned enough from experience that to "know thyself" is an extremely difficult and trying task, requiring repeated attempts. The same could be said for an organization or business. It is often difficult for those on the inside to gain an unbiased awareness of their own business.

Questionnaires

Questions are essential to the planning process. Some can be answered with an approximation, others you'll want to calculate carefully. Reviewing the answers to questions in the following areas will help you update your sense of "where you are."

Management Interest, Time and Aptitude

Interview yourself and your other principals about why you're not actively marketing life insurance in your agency. Answers you can expect to hear include:

- "We just have too many other balls in the air and just don't have the time."
- "We don't have enough in-house knowledge of life products and sophisticated life need selling so we stick with simpler needs - term and small permanent sales."
- "We've tried hiring a life specialist before and have just never been able to find the right person."
- "Our life specialist has become busy with group health and employee benefits accounts and doesn't end up producing much life business."
- "We have an arrangement with an outside firm who we bring in on larger life cases and that has worked out well. We don't want to do more than this."

Staff Skills and Interests

- What are the ages of the key owners and producers?
- Who has plans for retirement, and when?
- Do agency perpetuation plans need expanding or updating?
- Are we prepared for an unexpected death or disability (or defection) of one or more key people?
- Is our current staff fully utilized, with little or no time for new business even if it came in?
- Does anyone have time to research new options, learn, make new contacts, and grow professionally, or must we add people (or streamline systems?)
- Do the skill sets of our staff meet future requirements, or are there unmet or deferred training needs?
- Are individual talents optimally matched with "real" job descriptions?

- Do we have principals who must manage, but are really the best salespeople, etc.?

Company Relationships

- Are we representing the right companies?

- Could we do as well, or better, if we consolidated some business that is spread out now, into one or two strategic markets?

- Is there a company we could really grow a lot with, that we don't have access to now? How can we attract them?

- Do our key companies know how important they are to us?

- Do we really know what their objectives are in our territory for the next year or two?

- How could we improve communication?

Book-of-Business Analysis

Review accounts by their NASIC (formerly SIC) codes and by neighborhoods (zip codes, towns, counties, etc.)

- Does our mix of business, by class or by territory, vary in if we look at our newest (or oldest) clients? What classes are growing the fastest? Where is the most attrition?

- Business mix by account size and by line of business - large commercial, small commercial, business L&H, personal L&H, personal P&C - what's growing the fastest... the slowest? Why?

- What is our single largest account; what has been our biggest Life sale in recent years? Why did we succeed with these? Can we write more of them?

- Could we handle larger accounts? If so, how much larger - and what do we need to do to prepare for this change in scale?

- How many "orphan" (only one policy or service provided) accounts do we have in each class and line of business, and how many two-, three- and more- lines written accounts?

- How aware are we that we are in a race with the competitor writing other lines to get all the customer's business? (Are we acting in accordance with 1:1 Marketing principles?)

Systems Analysis

- Have we recently analyzed and optimized internal workflows? Is it time to begin (or expand) transactional filing? Are submissions and proposals always complete, attractive, and on time?

- Automation — is it time to start planning for a hardware or software systems upgrade? Are we taking full advantage of upload and download services provided by our companies? Is now the time to implement voice-mail, internal e-mail, external e-mail?

- Are we tracking the customer/prospect information that we'll need to? Do we know how many cross-sales we already have between Personal Lines, Commercial Lines and L&H? Why not?

- Does our system run our current jobs right? Is it adaptable to new tasks?

Data Analysis

- Do our principals regularly monitor, and act on, accurate periodic reports of our financial ratios and resources?

- Do we have adequate working capital, strong debt to equity ratios? Do we have a plan to improve or maintain them?

- Have we analyzed the long-term effects of trends in attrition rates, by class and value and age of account?

- Where have our recent successes been? Where is it most likely we can continue to grow?

- Have we gotten sophisticated at quantifying the value of individual customers? Do we know what customers are costing us money? Do we have a plan with regard to both valuable and expensive customers?

- Are we aware of the level of profitability by business segment - are we looking for opportunities to jump past fixed costs that are already being met (or close to being met) in certain departments?

Environmental Analysis

Once the strategic planners have taken a thorough inventory of the history, culture, specialties, strengths, and weaknesses of their firm, thought should be given to the opportunities that might arise from the interaction of them with the economic world they live and work in. This self-analysis might be likened to a farmer selecting the best grade of seed available before planting; though soil conditions, available sunlight, pests, time of year, expected rain, and other factors will impact the final harvest. Similarly, "environmental" factors must be considered in developing an agency growth strategy. As a beginning, we suggest a review of these potential influences:

- Local and regional economy — is it stable, declining, or booming?

- Area demographics and population trends

- Area housing and construction projections

- What industries are dying out, which have a chance to take off?

- What will be the impact on various customers and prospects of technologies already "in the pipeline?"

- Analysis of competitors — where are they strong? Where are they weak?

- What business needs are currently under-served in your marketplace?

- Job market — how reasonable is it for us to expect that we can attract energetic talent to the agency?

- Companies and products — do you have access to those that will serve you best?

In reviewing these matters, consider how they affect you now, and what the impact in the near-term and longer-term future might be. When you lose sight of these factors, you set your agency up to become a "buggy-whip" manufacturer in an "automobile" world. History is filled with examples of companies or in some cases, entire industries, that ignored obvious signs that the business environment was changing irreversibly. Consider, for example, the potential impact on the airline industry when the "picture phone" becomes an every-day appliance. Will perhaps, as some predict, one-third or more of the airlines' "business travel" volume disappear, as many more personal conferences are held remotely via video conferencing, with digital "surround sound" and 3-D images that give the sensation that the parties are virtually in the same room?

Directed brainstorming is the best tool to use at some point in these deliberations. To get you started, we recommend Peter Schwartz's *The Art of the Long View - Planning for the Future in an Uncertain World.* With help and direction from such a text, you can consider the possible impact of things like:

- The demographics of our aging society — where the age 85+ group is the fastest growing segment of the population

- The "digital revolution" - the convergence of multiple technologies in telecommunications, video, audio, and computer software and hardware

- The "commoditization" and universal availability of information — information on virtually ANY subject will be available from the Internet

- The globalization of trade and communication — our shrinking world

- The growing stress from an "information over-loaded" society (a CLU/ ChFC CEO survey found that about two-thirds of all executives suffer from information overload)

Plotting the Direction of Growth with Action Plans

With a careful self-analysis and environmental analysis well underway, a sense of direction will begin to arise from the facts of your situation. Now, rather than dashing off blindly into the future, your organization will be ready to make good decisions about putting the most resources behind plans that will bring the highest return. Instead of a "scatter gun" approach to cross-selling and cross marketing, planners will gain real clarity about what to sell, to whom, and in what manner. Keep in mind that many components of the "old model" will not fit the new situation. It probably won't be enough to "fine tune" or "polish" what you have always done.

No matter how good your service, how low your price, or how quick your response time is, such business practices can be duplicated by your competitors. In a time of rapid development in computers and communications, it is likely that your competitors will find ways of surpassing the best that you *used* to do. For a sustainable competitive advantage, you must truly add value to your customers' business (or to your personal lines customers' lifestyles). This critical point deserves an entire book, one which has in fact already been written — *Cooperate to Compete: Building Agile Business Relationships* by Preiss, Goldman, & Nagel. By making your organization, your people, and your contacts a part of the business and personal success of your clients, you position your business to ward off competitive threats from any quarter.

Some thought should also be given to an explicit statement of strategic direction. This is a "mission statement," but not in the traditional sense. Rather than being composed for an outside audience (customers, investors, prospects, vendors), the statement would be used to maintain the internal focus of the retailer's management. In a fast-changing environment, this brief document can be a "living" one — modified as required to adapt to new circumstances and opportunities. It should recognize where you are and what's going on around you, and then clearly state where you are going.

If the "Agency Self-Analysis" and "Environmental Analysis" studies outlined above have been completed, you have a good grasp of a core set of facts, including:

- Specific identification of your most valuable customers;
- Analysis of which customers have the best potential to become significantly more valuable;

- Ranking of vendor and insurance company relationships with respect to marketplace advantages for you today (and tomorrow);
- Identification of internal resources and strengths - sales talent, analytical ability, community connections, technical know-how, reputation, expertise in specific fields, etc.; and
- Knowledge of the demographics and economic trends in your marketing region.

Building on these facts, craft your strategic mission statement to acknowledge the following four objectives:

1. We will retain and strengthen our relationship with our most valuable customers.
2. We will develop those potentially valuable customers by gaining more of their business.
3. We will identify and focus new sales efforts on prospect groups that involve a three-way match: our talents, the prospect group's significance in our territory, and our advantageous relationships with vendors that target that group.
4. If we cannot accomplish the above three objectives due to lack of internal resources or external relationships, we will develop or acquire those resources and/or obtain or nurture those relationships.

Developing an Action Plan

In today's competitive economy, to "Strengthen our relationship with our most valuable customers" does not mean more shmoozing, more golf matches, or more fancy dinners. Business relationships today grow stronger when more and more important problems are identified (or even anticipated), and as elegant, cost-saving or revenue-enhancing solutions are provided. "Potentially valuable customers" are "developed" in the same manner — by providing more solutions to more problems than you have in the past. Gaining market share among new prospect groups is little different (but can be a bit more difficult) — retailers must demonstrate an attitude that says, "We can do this, and many other useful things as well: we can help you succeed in a number of ways."

That attitude is the attitude of cross-selling and cross-marketing. The capabilities to back it up must be in place, or be developed, and this may require specific action steps. To competently provide P&C insurance for a personal- or commercial-lines customer, you must know a lot about them and about their plans. This knowledge leads to awareness of problems and needs in other areas (such as Life, Health, Benefits, planning, Human Resources, etc.). By virtue of providing some P&C insurance, your organization already has the two most important elements for the sale of other products: the existing relationships of trust, and the knowledge of needs in other areas (or the ability easily to acquire such knowledge).

Action steps that will take advantage of these opportunities fall into three categories:

1. Develop or acquire or gain access to the expertise needed to meet those needs;

2. Establish or enhance relationships with the best vendors of products or services that will meet those needs; and

3. Activate the sales and marketing plan that will generate revenue streams from these activities.

Outsourcing vs. Internal Expansion

Note that in the action plan's first step (above), there are three options. It may not be practical or affordable for a small shop to develop life sales talent internally. Even a medium-sized retailer may not, at first, have the resources to attract and retain a top-flight benefits department. And even a very large P&C organization may find that it makes good business sense to "outsource" certain activities. It makes little difference to your customer (or to your sales relationship with that customer) whether you say "We have the people who can help you with that," or if you say "We can put you in touch with the best people in that field." The customer has the problem, and in either scenario, you have solved it for them.

Corporate boundaries are becoming more and more "fuzzy" as the advantages of networking, outsourcing, and strategic partnering become more apparent. A principal focus of the strategic planning process should always be on what you will do "in-house" and what you will get others to do for you. At a certain point in their evolution, most insurance retailers decide, as a minimum, to undertake both P&C and L&H sales and services internally. Other, closely-related activities may be brought in as operations reach a certain size, such as loss control engineering, or TPA services. They may be brought in, but this is not always the best option, even for very large operations.

Creating a new business division requires capital, involves risk, and dilutes top management's attention from other activities. Such activities always involve tradeoffs, the supporting of one corporate venture instead of allocating the resources used to another possible activity. Yes, if successful, a new "in-house" activity gets all of the revenue from the customer when that activity is performed, but at a cost. A real business decision must be made: would it be better to "partner" with someone we trust that is already and expert in that field, earning "finders fees" or other revenues from them in return for introducing them to our clients?

There is more than one mid-sized P&C agency with a pretty good L&H department that still outsources larger, self-funded group benefits cases to a specialist. Occasionally, even an experienced life producer will run across a very big, very tough case with a lot of competition and in such cases it makes sense to bring in a "big case expert" to assist in the underwriting and presentation of the account. The trick is to have an adequate variety of such relationships in place ahead of time, ready to respond as the opportunities come up, and to give the greatest care to maintaining the goodwill in such an arrangement. Often, establishing a written contract makes good business sense for both parties. Such an agreement would specify who "owns" the customer, how revenues will be shared, and what the responsibilities of the respective parties are.

If it makes sense to outsource some insurance and insurance-related services (and it often does), it is even more sensible to look to outside experts for "cross-marketing" opportunities. We'll explore these cross-marketing relationships in more detail in Chapter 6. For now, just consider how hard it is for your producers and service staff to get up to speed and stay knowledgeable in just the "limited" field of P&C (or L&H) insurance. It is virtually impossible for one person to attain and maintain high-level competence in both P&C and L&H insurance, let alone to do so in insurance and an unrelated field such as banking or human resources. The underlying idea in cross-marketing activities is to have available the best sources of other services (like equipment financing, or human resources data management) the client is likely to need, and to provide ready access to those services (for a fee from the customer or the service provider).

In other words, don't expect your people to have to become experts in every business field. Rather, insist they become expert at asking questions that identify customer and prospect problems and needs. Then, the job of the retailer's leaders is to negotiate lucrative relationships with vendors of products and services that will meet those needs, so that producers can "activate" those relationships as needed.

Bigger Can Be Better: the Power of "Clout"

Yes, size alone sometimes does make a difference, opening doors that would otherwise be forever closed to tiny operations. The second action step above (establishing and enhancing relationships with the best vendors) can sometimes be accomplished only by the larger and/or growing operations. Additionally, there are often "economies of scale" that make a $25 million book more profitable than five $5 million books. Certainly, it is easier for a sizeable regional agency to attract and maintain prestige relationships with the best underwriting companies than it is for the "mom & pop shop." So, even if you have your act together as a sales organization, you might still want to take a good look at merger or purchase opportunities. If you like the people, if your cultures are similar, if the pro-forma financials look good, consider it.

There are other alternatives available to insurance retailers less drastic than merger or acquisition. These include "agency clusters," affinity and marketing groups (like ARM International, Group 500 and Assurex), and franchises (like the ISU organization in Western states). To one degree or another, these organizations attempt, among other things, to give "clout" their members use with vendors, through awareness-building and lobbying efforts based on the size of members' aggregate book of business. The success of such activities seems to vary inversely with the degree of independence maintained by each group's members — if the group cannot back up a commitment (or a threat) with changes in member behavior, insurance companies are smart enough to see through the "story."

What About Acquisition as a Way to Grow?

The number of independent P&C agencies continues to decline, continuing a trend that started over two decades ago.[1] Landing new accounts is hard work. It takes good producers, and not many of us know how to recruit, train, or motivate them. It requires sales management, investment in automation, managing of vendor relations — isn't there an easier way? Why don't we just buy out Jones and Son over in the next town? They're in worse shape than we are... we could probably get it pretty cheap!

If you own an agency struggling to grow, thinking like this may be tantalizing (especially if you've never acquired another shop). You've heard it worked for some agencies back in the 70's and early 80's, and you read about some of the larger outfits today (Hilb, Rogal & Hamilton; Acordia; A.J. Gallagher, etc.) that are expanding as fast as they are only with a great deal of help from active acquisitions departments. Proceed with extreme caution into this area. The less experience you have in analyzing and buying other agencies, the more likely you are to make a serious or fatal mistake (ironically, the more experience you have, the more likely you are to remember how disappointing some of the results have been).

For most agencies, acquiring another only begins to make sense if yours is already a streamlined, efficient, dynamic sales-oriented culture enjoying steady internal growth. It can make sense to use debt or equity to acquire the specific multiple resources of another, usually including young and mismanaged sales talent, sustainable relationships with good long term clients, expertise in specific industries you'd like to add, and preferred relationships with carriers you'd like to grow with. Keep in mind that some of those young producers may walk out on you (or rebel against real sales management), and some of those clients may bail out on you. You might see your competitor take over that attractive industry segment, and then have that desired company cancel your contract — leaving you with nothing but personnel squabbles, bad public relations, negative cash flow and a lot of regrets. Insurance agency acquisition is not for the timid.

Possible Partners - "Insourcing"

In "activating a sales and marketing plan" (the third action plan step, above), an additional set of arrangements could be made similar to outsourcing — this could be called "insourcing." Just as your people are positioned to recognize customer needs that you can get others to provide (which leads to your outsourcing the business to the others), in a similar way others in non-insurance businesses have relationships with their customers who need insurance (and other core products of your business) — and they could be introducing their customers to you.

For example, there might be a local bank or investment firm that sees potential in the insurance business, but that is reluctant to make the investment required to establish an insurance division. It might make a lot of sense for them to introduce your producers to their customers. You know it takes a lot of money to find suspects, to develop them in to prospects, and to turn some of these into customers. You also know that your "hit ratio" goes way up when you are referred to or introduced to a prospective customer by someone that prospect respects. Why not set aside the money it would take to "cold call" and pay that as a finder's fee (perhaps new and renewal) to the referring organization in return for the quality introduction. In this way, the "insourcing" business (the bank or investment company) gains a stronger relationship with their customer, they also gain an additional revenue stream from that customer with very little capital or management investment. Your organization, at the same time, gets a new customer for a much lower cost of acquisition, and can thus afford to share some of the revenue with the correspondent partner.

Help from Consultants

It can be tremendously beneficial to bring in an outside party to help with various stages of the strategic planning process. If your operation has been stuck on a "plateau" for several years, or if there is a real divergence of outlook among key people in your shop, the fresh insights and energies that can arise from an outsider can make all the difference. However, the hard-core decision making required to select and implement the actual plan cannot be delegated or avoided. Accordingly, your key people need to be involved in every step of the process, and need to keep the consultant on track. It will be money down the drain if the consultant's recommendations fall outside the range of what your leaders are willing to undertake.

Also make sure to use someone who is already familiar with the industry. There's too steep of a "learning curve" in just understanding our business to get cost-effective advice from an unfamiliar outsider. A number of retailers have become disillusioned with consultants after their agency wound up training a couple of 30 year-old MBAs about our industry, only to have them return with conclusions and recommendations that bordered on the absurd.

Likewise, beware of anyone trying to make the strategic planning process look somehow "mystical" — they're just pulling your leg. Agency planning is a business process, part science and part art, and good results come from simply having a good moderator and/or project leader who knows how to ask the right questions and how to put together the answers.

ENDNOTE

1. A Conning & Company 1996 Survey, cited in the February 3, 1997 issue of *The National Underwriter Property & Casualty/Risk & Benefits Management Edition* cover story, by Victoria Sonshine Pasher, declares that agency ranks "will fall from 44,000 in 1996 to 38,684 in 2001 and 35,777 in 2006, for a drop of nearly 19 percent".

Chapter 5

Tactics for Cross-Selling Life Insurance

At this point, we hope that you have decided that it makes good economic sense to begin asking your clients and prospects about their L&H insurance needs, or to step up your efforts if you already are doing so. You designed the sales organization, everyone left has bought in to the dynamic selling culture, and you clearly expressed and activated a strategic plan. Top management strongly supports the concept of selling life insurance (and possibly related products) and has stated clearly that every (applicable) employee's overall performance will be partially measured by how they contribute toward this mission. Reward and consequence feedback elements — the carrot and the stick — and back up the message with action.

It is now time to delve into tactics and get rolling with some actual L&H sales. Where do you start?

In this chapter, we will lay out some of the tactics and techniques for cross-selling life insurance. We'll review the differences between the L&H sales relationship and the P&C realm. We'll also help you decide what specific products to sell, and to whom. Recognizing that the approach must vary for agencies of different sizes and client mixes, tips and suggestions will be directed to specific types of retailers. We'll talk about selecting producers for the L&H functions — in-house, outside recruits, and outsourced. Tactics for each type of producer will also be considered. Toward the end of the chapter we'll address the topics of how to reward life production and how to set goals and expectations for different classes of producers.

Tailoring the Cross-Selling System

In developing an approach to L&H cross sales, "one size" definitely does not "fit all." What works for the ABC agency may fail completely over at XYZ. The implementation of cross-selling activities must be tailored to each retailer's client base, marketing territory, and personnel. The way to design a successful campaign is from the customer base *backwards*. It will be necessary to return to the data gathered in the strategic planning phase, again analyzing the retailer's existing client base. Take a good look at who your customers are. What industries are they aggregated in? How many individuals work in them? How much of your personal lines book falls in the middle- and high-income population? (See National Underwriter's *Building An Affluent Clientele* by Russ Prince and Karen Maru File for additional information on developing a wealthy client base).

A lot of the information you need to establish a tactical life sales campaign already resides in your files or in your computer. Is there a lot of agriculture-related business in your book (or in your territory)? If so, consider the significant estate- and business-planning needs of today's large family and corporate farms. Do you handle professional liability for accountants and attorneys? These folks are regular consumers of larger life insurance products, as well as a source of networked referrals. How about physician groups or hospitals — who is writing the life and related insurance for the large numbers of employees there?

If your shop has a lot of manufacturing businesses insured, then your producers already know three, four, or more of the top officers at each one. How many of your clients are involved in partnerships or small corporations? Each one presents opportunities to talk about the business perpetuation solutions available through life insurance.

Remember, cross-selling activities do not just generate additional revenue. Cross-selling makes strategic sense because it gets your organization more involved with your most valuable customers, and thereby insulates you better from the competition. Sooner or later on the P&C side, someone will be able to offer a better price, more service, or improved coverage to your best customer. Your best defense (and the only sustainable one) is to have your customer and his or her employees tied to you through a variety of service relationships. Of course, you still must be reasonably competitive on the P&C side — but "reasonably competitive" will always be good enough if the customer recognizes you as a valuable business partner that can solve all kinds of problems.

Accordingly, your life sales campaign(s) should be directed first, and focused always, on your most valuable (or potentially valuable) commercial and personal lines customers. These are the ones you want to keep, that you want to keep happy. Identify them, and figure out a way to help them with their life insurance (and related) needs.

Overcoming the Obstacles

In Chapter 1, a variety of dynamics were uncovered which have, in the past, interfered with efforts to cross-sell L&H products in the P&C shop. At this point, we're ready to take them up again, and to jump over or dismantle them in light of the necessity of cross-selling activities.

Pressures on Your Staff's Time

The whole process of establishing a "sales system" (see Chapter 3) was to free up your producers, so that they could do what they do best — sell. Certainly, business conducted under older models prevalent in the insurance industry left little "free" time for selling of any type — as we saw before, the most successful producers ran out of time first (because they were expected to deliver all kinds of corollary "service" functions).

Now that workflows in your shop are redesigned so that P&C producers have time to sell, should they "go back to school" and become experts in the life and health business? Not at all. We'll see below that one possibility for developing life sales in your operation is to uncover and develop life talent in-house; a life "diamond" may be hiding in your P&C "rough." Once committed to that course, however, it would be unrealistic to expect that individual to maintain fluency with the broad and deep, rapidly-evolving field of P&C. There may be individuals trained in both medicine and law, but I don't want that same person to operate on my heart and to proofread my critical merger papers — at some point one needs focus, in order to gain the expertise expected of those in any professional field.

The amount of time our cross-selling system requires of the full-time P&C producer or CSR is only the time it takes to ask a few extra questions while meeting with or talking to existing clients or prospects. These are questions designed to uncover existing problems, with follow-up probes sufficient to have the prospect interested in hearing about solutions. At this point, though, we recommend that the producer or CSR say, "We can handle that - I'm going to have our business life (or estate planning, or employee benefits) expert stop in later this week."

Limited Access to the Most Competitive Products

Years ago, many P&C agencies only had access to a small set of L&H products, perhaps only those provided by one of their contracted P&C

markets. These products were typically not well-designed, flexible, or competitive. This is no longer the case. A retail shop with a solid L&H sales plan in hand and some real production talent can today find easy access to a full suite of extremely powerful L&H products and services. Life and related companies from around the world want nothing better than to get more effective salespeople actually selling for them. At the same time, the life offerings from traditional P&C companies have evolved, and many can stand head-to-head with the best from the life specialists.

One of the challenges today, in fact, is to select among the many options available. A certain amount of management time must be devoted to identifying and comparing markets in the L&H area, and in the negotiation of sales arrangements with them.

Shortages of In-house Technical Expertise

It is only realistic to expect that an agency's employment of, or access to, L&H sales skills and technical expertise will largely determine the type and extent of these sales which can be made. The section "Acquiring or Developing L&H Sales Talent" on page 97 deals with these challenges explicitly.

Cross-selling by in-house, cross-licensed P&C producers and CSRs will not extend beyond very simplistic, low-dollar sales — simple term sales with the occasional inexpensive permanent placement for a case where the need for life extends beyond 15 or 20 years. There could also be a handful of life payroll deduction accounts done with the help of a company specializing in this market, one that provides "enrollers" and some kind of streamlined underwriting and issuance process. (See National Underwriter's *Payroll Deduction: The Selling of Voluntary Benefits* by Walter B. Podgurski, CLU for more information on payroll deduction sales).

On the other hand, if there's in-house expertise or some outside relationship established, the only additional training required of P&C producers and CSRs is to ask about and to recognize "life" sales opportunities and buying triggers. As a part of the sales system, then, the retailer needs to have in place the methods and incentives for encouraging these leads to be passed on to the life producer or detached life relationship.

Inertia and Lack of Motivation

We've already seen how the mid-century models of insurance retailing cannot be sustained. Agency owners, managers, and producers who expect to prosper for more than a few years know that the motivation is already in place, for those who see it: *business survival.*

The rapidly changing business environment itself is a boon in that the buffeting it gives today's insurance retailer imparts a certain kinetic energy to those overcome by inertia. By shifting our perspective on events just slightly, we can see the rapidly-approaching future not as a threat, but as an exciting and meaningful challenge — something worth working for.

The Territoriality of Producers

This challenge, as much as any other, calls the retailer's top leaders to forge an unbreakable will, then to require fundamental change in both systems and attitude. Every business process, every system, and every employee must be directed to support sales — "sales" as newly and broadly defined; otherwise, all the talk of a new "sales system" and a "sales culture" will be only that — talk.

Your P&C producers may have thought till now that they "owned" the accounts they work on (in fact, by contract, they may have a vested interest in the ownership of them). If this proprietary attitude gets in the way of cross-selling and cross-marketing activities, leadership must change either that attitude, the assumptions that underlie it, or both. To be blunt, nobody (at your shop) will "own" anything if you lose your customers' business. To repeat: neither price, service nor coverage quality are sustainable competitive advantages. Only by providing more, customized, valuable products and services can you expect to achieve or maintain a long-term competitive advantage.

In some shops, tearing down the walls of these "fiefdoms" will be as radical a process as any arising out of this book. Stones in that wall that might need replacement include compensation systems, information systems, workflows, and sales team design. Sales "teams" are a good place to start, in fact. Some of the most successful P&C retailers never allow one person to call on (or to service) a significant prospect or customer.If a prospect is big enough to be valuable (or potentially valuable) to you organization, they are big enough to deserve a customized "team" of sales *and* service people.

When P&C producers are disabused of the idea that they "own" an account, then the argument that a life producer might "mess up" "their" account crumbles to dust. As we will see below, you don't want life sales and service people who are likely to "mess up" anyway. If you chose to develop a life sales functionality in-house, then these activities must become a "core competency" for you. If you select to outsource some or all of your L&H business, then you must undertake thorough "due diligence" and careful selection to get the right "partner" firm to work with.

While there are compelling reasons for divorcing producers from proprietary attachment to individual accounts, there are equally strong reasons for enabling key producers (and other key employees) to own part of the retailer's agency. We don't think equity should ever be *gifted* to employees, but for those who've proved themselves as valuable and committed, we do suggest that regular opportunities be provided for them to purchase, at a discount, with payments spread over time, some portion of (or stock in) the agency. In fact, it is unlikely you will be able to keep the best producers without providing meaningful access to ownership.

Then, when producers start thinking like part-owners of the agency rather than "owners" of a few accounts, the opportunities for cross-selling and cross-marketing will bloom in their hands. Your life producers may start wondering where their cold-calling time went, when the P&C salespeople keep taking them out to one "hot" customer after another.

Insufficient Automation Tools

Data analysis is a critical first stage of the strategic planning process; only in recent years have affordable agency management systems had the power to generate these reports. Sales force automation and marketing software, efficient word processing, and presentation management software all play major roles in the sales process today and will continue to in the future. With them, the best customers and prospects can be identified, and individualized marketing campaigns can be launched.

Cross-selling and cross-marketing a wide array of products and services to a large number of customers would be very difficult indeed without today's computers and communications tools. The life product illustration and sales process itself is fast becoming automated, animated, and graphical (see Chapter 7 for more on this). The simple function of asking "By the way..." kinds of questions can now be built into automated P&C sales and service call systems. The tools exist, and those who choose to pick them up and deploy them in dynamic L&H sales activities may do very well indeed.

Business Identity Barriers

The power and the responsibility of leaders is to define the situation and establish the identity of those following them. Verbal and behavioral cues can communicate what you think the organization is all about, and where it is going. It was natural, in days past, to say, "I'm an insurance agent. We sell insurance. We are a P&C shop." Experiment with different explanations of who and what you are, something like, "We are a financial services sales organization," or "We solve business problems for our clients," or "We help families manage their futures." When you find progressive alternatives that you're fairly comfortable with, start talking and acting in accordance with these subtle, but creative, changes in outlook.

Psychological and Sales Process Differences

If an office supply store began stocking and offering computers, software, and peripherals, its management would set up extensive training for the sales and service people, to make sure the investment paid off. Sales processes and techniques would need to be expanded — after all, the sale of a $3,000 computer is a different class of transaction than is the sale of a ream of copy paper.

P&C shops must expect to do no less: real training, serious coaching, follow-up, monitoring, feedback — all must be provided. Just hanging up a "Life Insurance" shingle will accomplish nothing. Everyone in the shop must be aware of the expansion, and must know enough about the objectives to recognize opportunities as they arise. Additionally, producers must be trained, and regularly "drilled" in the practice of asking more of the right kinds of questions. We suggest that the Sales Manager prepare a series of one-page outlines, containing questions regarding life and benefits needs that are applicable to various types of customers and insist that the questions be asked on sales and service calls.

P&C business customers and prospects often have business life insurance needs. These needs fall for the most part into three broad categories:

- Life insurance to fund a buy/sell or other perpetuation agreement;

- "Key Person" insurance to help the business survive until those few rare and special people that make the place profitable can be replaced — including not only the principals, but also key leaders, creative people, "rainmaking" salespeople, and skilled craftspeople; and

- Financial or balance sheet products for offsetting or eliminating debt obligations or lines of credit, mortgages, etc.

These needs represent tremendous revenue and loyalty-building opportunities, and can be among the easiest of sales, because most businesses with these needs are not acutely aware of them and have not insured them. All your people need to do is ask a few, well-planned questions to heighten this awareness — once the "pain" is felt, and they find out you can provide the solution, the checkbook comes out. Unlike the often tedious P&C sale, which almost always involves trying to take the account away from a competitor, you have no competition.

If your shop has a fledgling life department, but the life specialists there have not yet been trained in "business" insurance, these sales won't be quite as easy. Still, your clients will prefer to do business with your P&C agency for these needs — they already know and trust you. As your life people are trained and gain experience, we suggest that they approach these sales by forming relationships with outside life specialists who can lend their confidence and expertise on an "on call" basis. For many business life sales of moderate complexity, the underwriting life companies you are already doing business with will gladly send in a specialist or a team to assist in the product design, presentation, and sale (see the section on "Outsourcing").

Since the life sales process involves differences in sales psychology from that of the P&C sale, we recommend that P&C producers regularly make new, as well as service, calls in tandem with L&H sales staff. The value of "team selling" has already been discussed, but having a team composed of those with different backgrounds and different viewpoints can be even more valuable.

Once business life or other critical L&H needs have been identified, set up a "campaign schedule" so that someone from your organization is reminding them regularly of this unsolved problem. Repeat the same message to the client over and over again, in a variety of different ways — "persistence beats brains and sophistication every time." Give your prospect a variety of easy-response opportunities to keep the ball rolling. When you next make a "service-oriented" call, be sure that your employee remembers to say, "Oh by the way, are you ready to take a look at funding your buy/sell agreement as we've mentioned before?"

This can be a lot to keep track of, and when retailers reach a certain size a sales force automation software system may be required (see Chapter 7). Once that need is identified, find some way to make it automatic, for the next employee who has contact with the client, to pick up the dialogue right where it left off at the last time - "Did you have a chance to read that article about a split-dollar Life coverage we sent last month?" "What did your banker say about protecting that line of credit with some more Life insurance on your key people?"

The Trees and the Forest

Commercial P&C producers, when asked what customers they call on, will say "ABC Manufacturing, Community Hospital, and XYZ Wholesalers." Sales management must work diligently with these producers to correct this shortsightedness. These businesses are only half of the customer. The other half is "the president and controller at ABC, the physicians and other professionals at the hospital, and the partners and all the employees at XYZ." Earlier in the book, we deliberately turned the old phrase around and diagnosed this shortsighted view as being "unable to see the trees for the forest." Almost every individual employee and owner at every commercial customer and prospect location has a need for life and related lines of insurance. If your organization is not satisfying those needs, someone else (your competition) is, and they have a very large foot in the door that threatens your business relationship.

We recently talked to a P&C producer who asked the senior L&H producer from the agency to join him in talking with a commercial client who was reviewing their employee benefits program (which the agency did not write). It turned out that the controller had recently transferred in from another company, and the old company provided a considerable amount of group long-term disability coverage for officers, but that the current company did not. Arrangements were made to make a proposal to the finance committee late in the next quarter for similar coverage at this company. The P&C salesman was pleased, and started to close his notebook, when the L&H specialist asked, "Would you like us to get some LTD protection for you as an individual in the meantime?" The answer was a very enthusiastic "Yes!" Shaking his head on the way out, the P&C guy said, "Why didn't I think of that?" Of course, the next time something similar occurs, he will.

Balancing the Product Mix: What to Sell, What to Outsource

The L&H field is easily as broad and varied as the P&C side of the insurance business. It is a fairly rare (and usually quite large) L&H operation that has expertise and sales skill in every L&H sector. Here is the "short list" of product types, and the needs they can respectively meet, along with some marketplace notes, to give an indication of the scope of the field:

Life Insurance

Including a variety of Term products, Universal Life, traditional "Whole Life" (permanent), Term/Permanent blends, First-to-die policies, Joint and Last Survivor policies, Variable Life, Group plans

- Last expenses, mortgage protection, debt payoff
- Readjustment funds
- College education funds
- Programming needs and basic needs analysis measuring human Life value
- Life insurance to fund supplemental retirement needs
- Life insurance to fund estate tax liquidity
- Business Life needs (Buy-sell, Key Person, Deferred Compensation, Group Life, Group Life carve-out, etc.)
- Life insurance used in charitable contexts

Health Insurance

Including Small Group Medical, Partially Self-funded Group Plans, Family Major Medical, Long-term Care (group and individual), MSAs (Medical Savings Accounts), "Section 125" or "Cafeteria" Plans, Disability Income (short- and long-term, individual and group), Business Overhead Disability and Disability Buyout protection.

- Small group medical including managed care alternatives
- Individual major medical policies
- Long-Term Care as well as alternatives to LTC, and supplements to Medicare
- "Cafeteria" or Section 125 plans for flexibility and group employee appeal
- Income replacement in event of disability
- Funds to cover overhead expenses or buy out business in event of disability

Health insurance is a form of "must-have" insurance in the U.S. today, and is the most closely related of all the L&H coverages to P&C insurance. This similarity explains why many P&C firms offer some form of health coverage (individual and group) to their client base. Some P&C agencies even use small group health coverage as a "door opener" to get access to a customer's P&C business. The growth of managed care (HMOs, PPOs, etc.) has changed the face of medical insurance sales. Since 1997, the sale of small group health insurance has become much more challenging as underwriters tighten up due to new "guaranteed issue" and guaranteed portability issues in the new Federal law.

For two decades or more, the larger group medical area has been dominated by partially-self-funded plans, most of which combine specific and aggregate reinsurance with claims services provided by a third party administrator (TPA). Because of the high level of competition and variety of choices in this area, it makes sense for the retailer to stay in touch with, if not rely on, outside experts in this part of the market.

Long term disability (LTD) income coverage falls somewhere below health insurance from a "must-have" standpoint. Of all forms of life and health insurance, LTD is still the least penetrated market, especially for individuals and the employee groups at small and medium-sized businesses. Good quality LTD income coverage is fairly costly and too often prospective buyers cannot look beyond the cost relative to the monthly income that will be provided, and so choose to "retain" all or most of their real risk. In the back of their minds, many think they'll somehow be covered under Social Security for disability if it should strike; most haven't the slightest notion of how difficult it is to qualify for Social Security disability payments, or how low the benefits are.

Excluding from the averages all "blue collar" workers (who tend to have more disability claims), the chances of a "white collar" worker being disabled for more than 60 days prior to age 65 are about 1 in 25, according to a study by the U.S. Public Health Service several years ago. Even though this is far below the overall industry statistics typically cited which include the total population, those odds are still high enough that "retaining" the risk is still very "risky." Of course, if your client is the one out of 25 who experiences a long-term disability, statistics are meaningless — but your failure to sell the product becomes a source of regret for all.

The disability income sector of the insurance industry is in somewhat of a state of turmoil, due primarily to underwriting practices a few years back in the "professional" markets (such as coverage for physicians) where subjects were over-insured under non-cancelable policies (meaning the policyholder is guaranteed the right to renew, typically to age 65, and the company can't raise premiums during the period). Many carriers suffered major losses as a result, and have pulled out of the market; others have tightened up underwriting substantially, and/or are playing "hardball" at claim time. All of these factors can make LTD somewhat of a more difficult sale, and thus an area where using outside sales help could make good sense.

Annuities

- Fixed, Variable, Indexed - for all types of purposes
- Alternatives to CDs - Guarantee of principal - fixed and indexed
- Tax-deferred growth retirement planning vehicles - fixed and variable
- Variable annuities offer similarities to mutual funds with tax-deferred growth and "cost-included" built-in payout provisions

Annuities, both fixed and variable, have transformed the life insurance industry from being primarily "mortality-focused" into concentrating on "asset accumulation." Annuities will continue to expand in relative importance as "baby boomers" move through their top income years and continue to age, and will find the tax-deferred growth within annuities, both fixed and variable, a very attractive feature. The popularity of variable annuities will, to a large extent, be driven by the state of the stock market — up when it's up, and flat to down when it's down. Nevertheless, even when the variable products are "down," many of those "variable" dollars migrate back over to fixed annuities, and/or to the new "indexed" annuities which have stronger "downside" protection.

Qualified Plans

- 401(k)s
- Defined Contribution and Defined Benefit Pension and Profit-sharing plans, Keogh plans
- SEP IRAs
- Simple IRAs and more

It won't be realistic to expect that any one L&H producer (or even the whole department) will be able to develop world-class expertise in all the above sub-specialties. It does make a lot of sense, though, to train them to uncover and develop needs in all these areas. Then, the question becomes simply, "Can we handle this in-house, or do we bring in an expert from one of our correspondent outside partners?"

Acquiring or Developing L&H Sales Talent

Part of the answer to that last question hinges on who you have working for you. If you are committed to insurance retailing as a core activity of your business, you'll want to have at least a basic set of L&H capabilities in-house. It doesn't make much business sense to farm out what you are supposed to be best at; rather, keep sight on the objective of getting even better at your main business, and manage the special opportunities "by exception." Gradually work your way into more and more insurance sales sub-specialties, learning from the real experts along the way. Treat these business mentors fairly, pay them well, and be up front about your interest in growing more into their area of expertise, and you should be able to keep everyone happy.

Finding People In-House

To review, there is a big difference between uncovering a problem and fixing it. Everyone in your organization should have the "basics" of asking questions inculcated into their work routine. This includes CSRs and producers who have in the past been the most "life-adverse." For all but the L&H specialists, though, the next step is a "hand-off" to the life department — if you have a life department.

If you've decided to market life, health, and annuities internally with your current group of producers and CSRs, you must accept the fact that this is a huge undertaking and long-term in nature. Yes, near-horizon technology will help, stepping the relative novice through automated, interactive sales presentations and guiding product choices with "expert underwriting systems." Historically, though, most attempts to get existing P&C producers to actually make life sales, other than pretty simple and obvious ones, just haven't worked.

If you think there is some hidden "life talent" in your organization, a practical first step would be some simple, inexpensive testing, to ascertain the degree of compatibility with the psychological profile needed for a life sales career. It would be unusual, but not unheard-of, for a great P&C salesperson to also succeed in the life field. One indicator worth noting would be the P&C producer that seems to be developing a pretty good book of group medical clients — this person may have that special personality needed for big success in the life sales field.

If you've already invested a good bit in a P&C producer that is not meeting minimum goals, but you like having them around, why not try some testing to discover if there could be some predilection for Life sales, before you fire them?

Recruiting and Training New People

Realistically, we have seldom seen a "life superstar" come over from the P&C ranks. The best success stories involve taking a new agent, not already set in his or her ways, and thoroughly indoctrinating him/her in all facets of life insurance. The problem for all but the largest retailers, is that the training on the life side must come from somewhere, and the small and medium-sized agency is not equipped to undertake this specialized training internally.

Most P&C shops, therefore, recruit life specialists who have received experience and training outside the agency. It is not at all unusual to find someone with five, ten, or more years of successful sales experience with one of the "big" life companies like Prudential or Metropolitan who are frustrated with their situation. A P&C retailer is very well positioned to attract such people, since you can offer more freedom and flexibility, great support systems, a constant stream of good leads, and a wide variety of markets and products for them to sell (and perhaps a chance to buy part of the agency in time).

As you look, start to develop a good mental picture of this addition to your sales team. Consider these points:

- What have they achieved? (years in business, activity and sales levels)?
- The "wrong person can't make the perfect plan work, but the right person can make an imperfect plan work"
- You need a team player, not a lone wolf
- Degree of technical competence required for your client base
- Years of experience, degree of "social polish"

Once you've located a possible recruit, proceed carefully. Strongly consider background checks, demand (and consult) several references, require more than one psychological profiling test, and have several formal interviews and less formal meetings — both with other front line P&C and L&H producers as well as with your top management.

In your meetings and interviews, be looking and listening for things like these:

- Does he or she use the word "we" and "you" as much as "I" (Life producers need a little more empathy and a little less ego than a P&C producer)
- Do you pick up on a high sense of urgency, a mission in life, the wish to accomplish something?

- Are there any signs that a high sense of integrity and ethics are lacking?

- Can this person strike a good balance between being client-sensitive while still taking care of the necessary details and paperwork?

- Is the recruit looking for a "nest" in your office, or do they love the life of beepers, mobile phones and automobiles?

Outsourcing Some (or All) of the Life Sale

We've already seen that all but the largest life departments have to outsource some of their most technical sales challenges. At the same time, other P&C retailers may find the prospect of staging a full-blown L&H department too daunting, or they may have other strategic opportunities that are taking most of their time. In other words, at some time or another we all will need to farm out some (if not all) of our L&H opportunities. You should give as much care to selecting and negotiating with these "outsiders" as you would in hiring an internal producer.

Just as prudent agency owners incorporate "non-piracy" language into their employment contracts with their producers, so should they be circumspect with outside "partners." We know of more than one case where the life part of a really good account was referred to a trusted correspondent business, who turned around and co-opted the entire business, thumbing their noses at the originating agency.

Using an outside "life partner" can frequently work for P&C shops that already have a very productive group/benefits department specialist, who is less comfortable with sophisticated life sales.

So what are the things you should look for in setting up an arrangement with an outside "Life partner"- whether an individual or organization? We suggest attention be given to these attributes:

- *Professionalism* - the agent or agency you bring in will be representing your firm; although you know they're separate and distinct, if you bring them in, your client thinks of them as you. For starters, the Life Partner (or many on their staff) should have his or her CLU (Chartered Life Underwriter), and preferably the ChFC (Chartered Financial Consultant) and/or CFP (Certified Financial Planner) designations.

- *Proficiency* - Are they keeping current? Ask whether they are PACE-certified, meaning if they're a CLU or a ChFC, have they made a professional commitment to a certain number of continuing education credits over the 2 year certification period? CFPs also have minimum CE standard that must be met in order to continue using the designation.

- *Integrity* - Although you can't touch or smell it, you can sense it. Just to be sure, ask around, get some references, and check them out. It might make sense to do a professional background check on some people — just be up front about your plans to do so.

- *Ownership of the Client* - Now is the time to have some frank discussions about the third party's role, and how they will be expected to deal (or not deal) with the client assuming a sale is consummated.

- *Commissions and Fees* - You can be at a business disadvantage if the third-party "life partner" agent writes the business totally in his or her name, while paying you a portion of the commissions and/or overrides (Note: be careful of state regulations here, there must be a licensed life agent within your P&C agency involved in these hand-off transactions). Over time, the servicing of the business may very likely fall back into your hands, and if vested renewals are paid to the original writing agent, you may be unable to transfer servicing to them. Nothing can be more frustrating than to be servicing life business for one of your clients, while receiving no renewal commissions, knowing that the "outside" life agent (who has by now perhaps retired) is getting them all.

On the other hand, the outside life partner, by virtue of their doing significant business with a certain underwriting carrier, may be able to bring a healthy override and office expense allowance to the table. Assuming the P&C agency (or principal) is contracted as a "broker" and a party to the case, there can often be more of a total "pie" to be split up. In those cases where your client was already "sold" on the life purchase, your originating agency can often negotiate to receive the lion's share of the income from such a case. In such a situation, the life partner will realize they are really only being brought in to deliver the final product, and few costly services. Another point — don't just negotiate first year commissions; remember the renewal income, and be frank and realistic about who is going to do the actual service work on the business over time.

It used to be that other than an occasional request for a change of beneficiaries, most life business didn't carry much of a "servicing" responsibility. That is no longer the case. In today's "due care and diligence" and "illustration integrity" world, someone better be supervising the entire life cycle of each policy sold through your shop. Keeping in mind the example of all the class-action suits on "vanishing premium" life sales made during the 1980s, don't take these responsibilities to your customers for granted. Clients have been known to have "selective memories" and getting "in-force ledgers" done every couple of years is just a part of doing business these days. Be sure, whether the business is all internal or involves a life partner, that someone is minding these details (and that these responsibilities are clearly contracted).

Outsourcing the "Special Case": Finding Expertise in Underwriting

The alert (or lucky) producer at any retailer will uncover a really big life case every now and then. It might be a $15,000,000 estate tax "problem," a $10 million need to fund a buy-sell agreement, or it might be a high-tech company needing to insure the lead scientist responsible for almost all the company's products and growth. It may be ironic, but most of these cases involve significant medical underwriting challenges. For instance, many of the larger cases involving business or estate owners will need to insure persons in their 50s, 60s, 70s, or even 80s. Show a life underwriter five 60-year olds worth over $2 million each and we'll bet you at least one of them will have a serious health problem or history, that one or two more will present some questionable underwriting areas, and only one or two will turn out to be "preferred" clean risks.

Similarly, business owners, especially those who have built a successful business from scratch, often pay a high price with their health ("workaholic" stress-related illnesses abound in this group).

So what do you do when a huge need exists along with great opportunities, but the underwriting challenges are beyond your experience? Now, no matter the size of your operation, is the time to call in some high-level help. Using an outside agent experienced in these type of cases or using a "brokerage agency" that specializes in these types of cases can make all the difference in "landing" the business.

There is no better alternative in such situations than bringing in a sophisticated life partner, one who can communicate with the senior underwriters and the physicians involved. If the "impaired risk" client is not properly assessed or is not prepared for the potential rating, it can not only blow the case, but can ruin your entire relationship with the client. Don't let greed tempt you to overreach your capabilities. Ignoring this advice, you'll miss out on these opportunities — you may get started, you may convince the prospect that life insurance is the best solution, but your prospect will ultimately place their business with someone who can operate at the lofty levels that are required. It can take some time to locate and develop the relationship required with these heavy-hitters, but it is well worth the effort. Just one successful placement at this level can turn a so-so year into a resounding success, even when revenues are shared with the expert.

The larger estate planning cases are in many ways the most profitable cases any retailer can sell. Many of these cases involve tens and even hundreds of thousands of "annual" life premiums. These sales are often conceived and promoted by an estate planning attorney and/or CPA. As a long-term strategy, it would make sense to identify and start working with some of these professionals. A good place to start is by referring some of your customers to them, instead of asking them to refer to you. If you begin a business relationship by demonstrating that you are willing to give, to contribute to the other outfit's success, things are likely to start happening that will help you.

Such professionals will, of course, feel more comfortable recommending you if you have a professional in-house life specialist. If you have established a regular working relationship with an outside professional "life partner," you'll want to find a way of communicating this advantage to the CPAs and attorneys.

These estate planning challenges involve changing the prospect's perception of life insurance. Instead of viewing it as an "expense," the most successful life agents guide such prospects into seeing how the life product can be a financial "leveraging device" — paying pennies in premiums per year for each dollar of death benefit.

Because the estate liquidity sale involves the entire family, and because it's a very emotional sale where procrastination tends to be the number one enemy (i.e. many of these cases die in "mid-air" due to lack of follow-through, change in a client's situation, or just plain stubbornness), patience and persistence are demanded of the sales organization. Often, these cases take 6 months to a year (or longer) to close, from the time they are opened up to when a policy is finally underwritten and put in place.

Life Sales Approaches

Many types of life insurance sales involve an almost completely emotional purchase. When you get right down to it, the consumer buys a product that is not going to be needed (excluding access to cash values) until they have departed this world. No one can predict in the future who will: 1) live far beyond average life expectancy; 2) live just to approximate life expectancy; or 3) die long before actuarially expected. Therefore, a consumer's decision about when to purchase life insurance offers a wonderful (and often adopted) opportunity for procrastination. Consequently, the life sales system in your operation must have built-in reminders and follow-ups. No one likes to be a "nag," so let your computers do it, reminding your life producers to ask, and ask again, and to keep on asking, sending out stuffers, mailing out letters, and prompting CSRs to make telephone calls.

Many types of life insurance are not purchased for one's self, but for those who will survive; as a "selfless" purchase, the motivations of "character" and love must be uncovered. Sensitivity, empathy, and the ability to arouse these sentiments are required at several points in the development of a life sale.

Some forms of life insurance involve more tangible needs, and therefore are easier to sell. For instance, life insurance to pay off a mortgage is a "natural" adjunct to a homeowners policy sale. Asking for the life insurance should be automatic with all your personal lines staff.

One elusive, yet important, concept that must be communicated in many life sales situations is that of the prospect's "human life value." This concept, developed by Solomon Huebner, founder of the CLU and ChFC movement, recognized the income-generating potential of a human over his or her entire projected working lifetime. For some prospects, the use of good "needs analysis" software programs can be used to illustrate the concept. A less formal approach is to use a "rule of thumb" formula, whereby a person "should" be insured for 5-7 times his or her annual income. In one way or another, the life producer must at some point convey the pure "economic value" of the prospect's life, as if he or she were a "money-manufacturing machine," cranking out $50,000, $100,000,

$200,000 or more per year. Then, factoring in inflation and career advancement, some truly impressive numbers can be generated to communicate the need for insuring that machine in the event of a "breakdown."

Some individuals, when presented this concept, want to insure themselves for whatever it would take to allow their family to maintain an equal (or better) standard of living at their death. Others will still only want to cover some very short-term needs of the survivors (i.e., enough for funeral expenses, perhaps to pay off the house, and maybe a couple of years income to get the family through a re-adjustment period).

Every life prospect will have a unique set of priorities; what's true for one person will not be true for the next. Keep in mind that these priorities tend to shift over a life customer's lifetime. For example, the need to set aside substantial funds for retirement does not usually "hit home" until most people reach their 40s or 50s. The need for long-term care protection usually becomes apparent when one of the aging parents goes into a nursing home and the associated costs begin mounting up.

Figure 5-1 illustrates that for some "average individual". . .at this particular point in his or her life, *where* these various needs might fall along a horizontal axis where the far left represents "Must-have Insurance" and the far right indicates coverage which the person perceives to be "Nice-to-Have," or even unimportant. Although varying from individual to individual as well as changing over time, it is nevertheless a useful exercise to find out in an early interview where curent or potential clients they would place themselves along this continuum.

Figure 5-1

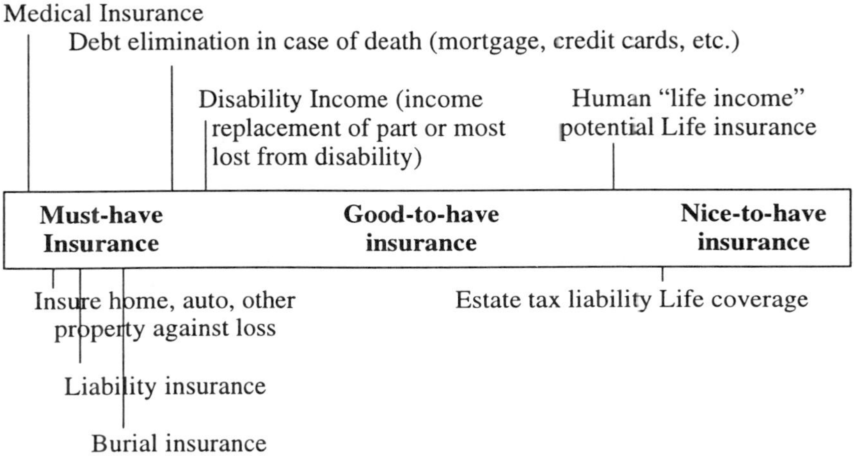

A good way to determine where a person falls regarding their "philosophy of *life* insurance" is to use a traditional "needs-based" insurance selling cycle, which can be described as including four basic steps:

1. *Identifying and uncovering needs.* No salesperson can create a need. It either exists, or it doesn't. If there is no need identified, the salesperson should go on to the next prospect. A lot of time has been wasted by salespeople trying to impose non-existent needs on prospects. However, it is not at all unusual for real needs to exist, outside of the awareness of the prospect, or for needs to be much more serious than the prospect thinks. This leads to the next step, one that requires a great amount of life selling skill.

2. *Creating a sense of urgency to solve that particular need today.* This is the essence of salesmanship — overcoming the natural human tendency to procrastinate and/or to rationalize. The most successful sales people "fact-find" early in a sales call interview, and use these facts as a basis for asking questions that probe for real needs implicit in those facts. Further probing is required to develop an appreciation of the true scale of the problem, and to create a sense of urgency in the prospect's mind. At this point, the reuse of the personalized information gathered earlier is incorporated into the products presentation to personalize and add weight to the sales process.

3. *Presenting the product and/or service in a positive light.* Once awareness of the problem(s) have been built to the point that the prospect wants to solve it, presentation involves the relatively simple task of communicating how your solution will solve the problem. The focus, then, at the presentation stage is on the "details" focusing on various options and add-ons: "Do you want the big one, or the smaller one?" or "Do you want to pay annually, or would monthly be better for you?"

4. *The Close.* For the most successful salespeople in any field, there is no "close" at the end of a sales presentation. The close begins when the first piece of information is gathered which hints of or points to a specific need, continues with developing that need into a felt desire, and is concluded by illustrating and

personalizing the solution for the prospect's individual situation. The conclusion of the most successful sales process, rather than being a traditional "close," is a discussion of alternatives and options, wherein you ask the customer finally "OK" their choice with a pen on the application.

A Note on "Objections"

If real needs exist, then of all the possible objections that can come up during or at the end of the sales interview, the only one which really counts (except for a legitimate "no money") is "lack of trust." Lack of trust manifests itself in many other objections: "I want to wait and think about it a little more"...."I want to look around some more" ...and on and on, but assuming a genuine need has been identified and there's genuine agreement that it does exist, lack of trust is most often the real culprit.

That's one of the key advantages that P&C agents have in selling life or other forms of insurance. Due to the nature of the P&C relationship (i.e., it's more of a must-buy purchase) and because of the different sales approach of the typical P&C agent (i.e., more laid back, more analytical, not as high-pressure or emotional), there tends to be a higher degree of comfort and trust inherent in talking with the P&C agent than would be with an unfamiliar life agent.

Asking the Questions, Staying in Touch, and Responding Promptly

Training all your people to routinely ask questions that will uncover needs for L&H insurance has already been emphasized. We remind you again of this necessity, though, and suggest that you find ways to regularly remind your co-workers (and to quantitatively evaluate their compliance).

For life sales in particular, though, the question or the reminder must come to the prospect's attention at the right time. The "right time" is when a "life change event" has occurred — a major development in the prospect's personal or business life. Such events include:

- marriage
- birth of a child

- graduation from high school or college
- divorce
- death of family member, partner, or close friend
- formation (or expansion) of a business
- job change or promotion
- home purchase, other major asset acquisition, or the incurring of major debt

In order to be the one your prospect turns to when such things happen, there must have been a certain level of awareness built in their mind over time. This awareness grows not only with your staff's questions, but also through advertisements, invoice "stuffers" and "mailers" (more on these in the Appendices), business signage, articles you write, speaking engagements you participate in, and other activities. Remember that a top-level commitment is needed to succeed big in the L&H business, and this includes a commitment to spend time and money on a well-rounded, extensive, and on-going marketing program.

A very important quality to build into your life sales and marketing system is *responsiveness*. Once your customer or prospect has indicated any interest at all, your system must be poised to immediately jump at the opportunity. Delays of even a day or two in responding can sabotage a sale or give your competitor a chance to gain a foothold on your customer. When an incoming request is received or a possible need is uncovered, specific "triggers" should automatically be activated that make it automatic for a phone call and an appointment immediately to follow.

How Should You Compensate a Life Producer?

One of the most difficult aspects in attracting and retaining a good life producer is how to set up a compensation package which will be fair and advantageous to all parties. Potential earnings will need to be significant enough to attract and motivate a top quality person, and the retailing organization must also expect profits from the arrangements (in addition to the customer-loyalty gains arising from account rounding).

There is no single compensation system which will work for all P&C agencies and for all situations. This also implies that it should be made clear up front that the compensation arrangement will periodically be monitored, and may be changed, to make sure it's still meeting the requirements of both parties involved.

Make sure that any prospective life producer coming in from a life-only organization understands the value that he or she will derive from a steady stream of introductions and leads from your staff. This type of lead represents "found" business to the life specialist, and he or she should recognize that fewer cold-calls and a higher closing ratio will translate into more revenues for all. Also, if the retailer will be providing office space, equipment, reception and secretarial help, cars, employee benefits, and the like, the life producer should be made aware of their cost to the agency. Both "free leads" and "paid support services" mandate a lower commission split for the producer than would exist otherwise.

The life specialist should be expected to bring in consistent business of his or her own. It's not a "one-way" street and you don't want to attract someone who only sees you as a way to get out of the "prospecting" business. A mediocre agent who was already slowly failing out of the life business almost never works inside a P&C agency.

We recommend a mutually-reinforcing compensation system that rewards internal referrals. When a P&C production and service team introduces a life producer which leads to a L&H sale, the P&C people should be paid a part of the revenue from that business. A similar arrangement should compensate L&H (or a personal lines, or accounting department) employees providing introductions or leads resulting in new commercial P&C business. Commercial L&H and P&C people should always receive recognition and a modest finder's fee for bringing in new business.

In addition, a spirit of co-operation should exist so that on large referrals of any type, customized arrangements can be negotiated among the various departments that fairly recognize the amount of work the parties will have to do.

The biggest mistake that some agencies make is that they inadvertently structure a compensation system which discourages attracting above-average or top-flight life producers. Depending on the support services and benefits provided, it might make sense for the agency to split revenues anywhere from 30/70 to 70/30. Sometimes a straight split will work out, in other cases agencies may allocate new and renewal commissions differently depending on producer involvement in ongoing service requirements.

However, if your prospective life specialist routinely writes a few $50,000 or $100,000 annual premium life cases every year (on his or her own "personal" clients), he or she might think twice about "giving" half or more of this income to an agency for overhead. As an incentive to work on larger cases, one option would be to "step up" the proportion paid to the producer for those cases that would have been in the top ten percentile by size of those he or she wrote the prior year (or for producers new to you, use sales above a certain size threshhold, which might be $5,000 or $10,000 or $25,000 in first-year commissions depending on the experience of the producer).

This type of sliding scale arrangement recognizes that the retail agency won't have much more fixed or variable costs to carry in support of a large sale than they would for a smaller one. Absent an extra incentive like this, a life producer might be tempted to leave the agency as soon as a jumbo case like this materializes.

On the other hand, if the life specialist is doing many small term cases, even if they're producer-generated prospects, relative costs per sale can be rather high (although automated underwriting systems can help here). Similarly, individual and group medical cases can involve more service and support dollars than most life policies; we know of several agencies that pay a smaller percentage of revenues to the L&H producer for health cases than for life sales.

Although it can be argued that the life specialist will benefit more from the number of large cases written on clients of the agency and therefore should be content with the lower split on ALL business, it usually makes sense to provide some flexibility and pay a higher percentage on very large premium life cases that the life specialist brings in on his or her own. The important point here is that the higher percentage paid to the life producer on larger life sales enhance the recruitment and retention of higher quality life specialists. Many top life producers, those who would make the most money for the agency, would see the much lower "traditional" compensation split as being unacceptable.

The most important ingredient for a successful life operation is having top-quality sales personnel, so remain flexible, and don't let short-term greed blind you to the future opportunities such people can bring to your organization. There are hidden benefits to the retailer that arise from having such stellar L&H people, including higher retention of P&C business where L&H has helped them, image and profile in the local and industry community, and contributions to overall energy and professionalism in your organization.

Here's an example of a "sliding" commission arrangement that can be the best answer. On larger cases generated entirely by the life specialist, a schedule for splits might look something like this:

Annualized Life Premium	Life Specialist	Agency
$10,000 - 24,999	60%	40%
$25,000 - 49,999	70%	30%
$50,000+	75%	25%

A couple of notes are in order. When these large accounts are originally generated from referrals or introductions from the P&C side, the incentive bonus or finder's fees payable to the P&C people come out of the L&H producer's part of the split, not the agency's. So, in the case of a new $50,000+ annualized Life premium sale initiated by a P&C producer, the L&H producer might receive 65%, the P&C producer 10%, and the agency still gets 25%. Second, it should be noted that these "annual" or "annualized" life premium numbers exclude "rollovers," "dump-ins," or "excess premiums." This is annualized ongoing level premiums on which full "base commission rates" are paid.

Once again, these numbers are certainly negotiable based upon the total package provided by the agency but the object is to fashion a compensation system that allows you to attract top quality life producers rather than mediocre ones that just view your agency as the "gravy train" that can take them out of the "prospecting" business.

Another advantage in attracting top-notch high volume life producers into your retailing operation is that some higher compensation contracts may become available based upon the producer's proven track record.

It is an entirely different situation dealing with an expert from the outside (a "Life Partner") rather than with an employee. Although it could be argued that you do not have to provide business space, receptionists, phone or other office expenses and therefore can afford to be more generous, it should be easy to negotiate no less than a 50/50 split of the compensation as a starting point. Then, based upon the relationship and the size of the case, you may wish to negotiate for a portion of the life partner's override or other revenues as well.

Typically, the better the life producer or life partner, the more he or she will want to have some input on carrier selection and to perform the due-diligence on the company and product selected, especially in light of today's tenuous legal environment.

How Much Life Production is "Enough?"

There's no easy answer to this question. Just as there are agents that write 300 cases a year, some succeed in writing only 30 a year; in some instances, the one writing 30 cases can create more revenue and significantly more profit than the one writing 300. From an industry statistics standpoint, about 50 lives a year has been identified the number which most life agents write in a year's time — roughly one per week. If a good number of these are significant cases, the revenue stream can be substantial. If all of these are basically small to medium-sized "term insurance" cases, something isn't working right. For a life specialist who usually writes medium sized cases and occasionally a few big ones, 100 life cases a year (2 per week) is an above-average job and 150 (3 per week) should make everyone happy.

If the agency has a heavy concentration of good commercial accounts, expectations for an experienced, talented life producer would range from several hundred thousand to over a million dollars of annual revenue. This is a fair assumption, and would vary mostly with the size and wealth of your client database. These projections also assume you aren't burying the life producer with less productive cases. A top producer in a situation like this would be primarily writing large estate and business cases, and while they might only write 15 to 25 cases a year, no one should be complaining.

When life agents do fail it is usually for one very simple reason: they aren't holding enough interviews with qualified prospects. If agents would forget for a moment that they are in the insurance business, and instead pretend they were running a manufacturing company, they might be better prepared for what they must do to survive and prosper. On the manufacturing side, you have to always be concerned with monitoring three separate but "closely integrated" areas: raw goods, goods-in-process, and finished goods.

Failure to carefully monitor any of these three items either results in "too much demand" and depleted inventories with no goods to sell, or all the raw stock getting into the pipeline and the next time you look back, you're totally out of raw goods. A point of emphasis: it all starts with raw goods. Raw goods in the life business can either be "suspects" or "prospects." A *suspect* is an unqualified name who may or may not turn into a *prospect*. We'll define a prospect as anyone with whom you've developed a tie of any kind.

Suspects can be anything from a name off a mailing list or out of a phone book, to a person or company whose name you saw in a local newspaper or magazine article. They become a "prospect" either when they respond "positively" by returning a reply card, responding favorably to a telemarketer's call, or when referred by a client. The strongest prospects are either a current customer or a referred lead. The strongest referred leads are those referred to you by a client who tells you they want to call their friends and/or business associate and then proceed to arrange a meeting with you because they are so impressed by the service you've provided. With "referred leads," it takes far fewer prospects as raw goods to end up equaling the same number of sales coming out of the factory.

Your Sales Manager should make sure that all three parts of the production "pipeline" are always adequately loaded, for each L&H producer. Weekly reports should detail the number of prospects (raw materials), the number of sales and applications in underwriting, and the number of issue (goods in process) and approved cases, and finally how many policies awaiting delivery (finished goods) there are. With good "inventory and production management, "sales slumps" can be eliminated.

Although there are any number of excellent prospecting and client management systems on the market today, one of the best and simplest ways to monitor this whole process is to set up a New Business Tracking Log either on a word processing system or spreadsheet software. It should be updated on a daily basis and reviewed weekly by whomever the life specialist reports to. These reports should contain enough detail to keep the names of the prospects, classifying them as to the potential size and "quality" of the lead.

By selling L&H insurance and services to your most valuable clients and prospects, you will have a better retention ratio, more loyalty, more revenue per account and per sales call, and more profits at the end of the year. We've seen that these goals can be accomplished with added (or retrained) employees, whose strengths are supplemented from outside "life partners" when high-level specialized expertise is needed. We have called this process "cross-selling." In the next chapter, we will apply these same principles to the "cross-marketing" of products that fall outside the traditional insurance product mix, and get an interesting glimpse of the exciting future for insurance retailers in the process.

Chapter 6

Cross-Marketing of Related Services

Once top management at a P&C retailer has ascertained that a sales culture truly pervades the operation, and that a dynamic sales system has been designed and activated, the foundations are in place for expanding sales activities beyond the traditional. In the context of the strategic planning process, life sales (as well as benefits and health program sales) were seen to be a first logical step for expansion. After all, L&H products are insurance products, and the introduction of them to our portfolio can occur with relative ease.

However, this strategic decision to "sell something else" was not a haphazard one. We "sell something else" because of our elemental sales sense, which recognizes that:

Valuable customers are retained when the sales organization uncovers or anticipates, and satisfies, a variety of customer needs, in a manner that consistently furthers that customer's goals and success.

If you need a pack of gum while traveling through Poughkeepsie, and find one at a convenience store a few blocks off the Interstate, you would not necessarily become that store's customer for life. In contrast, if there was a local emporium in your home town that delivered your groceries, videos, prescriptions, and picked up your dry-cleaning, and provided those products and services reliably and professionally, adapting their deliveries to fit in with your schedule and lifestyle, you would be very likely to remain a long-term (and valuable) customer of theirs. The difference is in scale, in the number of needs consistently met.

We have seen that "rounding out" an account with additional lines of insurance accomplishes two important objectives. First, as explained above, by assisting the customer in more than one way, the relationship between that customer and our sales team is strengthened, and our potential competitor's relationship is weakened. Secondly, in "selling something else," we have increased revenues per customer. In almost every case, this additional money from the same relationship is obtained more efficiently, thus more profitably, than would be the same sale to a brand new customer.

Earlier, in analyzing the insurance product and the role of the retailer, we found that in most instances the agent adds value (both to the customer and to the insurer) by selling and by communicating information — answering the customer's and the underwriter's questions. The retailer does not "make" the insurance product, and does not have to know everything about it — we let the insurers take care of the details of product design and delivery. In a sense, we're putting the customer in touch with someone else, who can bring to bear the systems and resources the customer really needs.

Once this somewhat humbling realization is absorbed, we can make the transition to selling products other than P&C insurance much more easily. The first step was the expansion into L&H lines. The next step, one already initiated by many agencies, involves the "unbundling" of the insurance product to provide customized components designed for each particular customer. Insights gained through this activity will lead many to the alternatives to traditional insurance as outlined below. Rather than stop there, however, as even the more progressive retailers have, we will prod the reader to depart completely from paths taken before, to step beyond the traditional boundaries of the insurance industry, into the "cross-marketing" of even non-insurance products.

"Cross-Marketing" Other P&C Products

It may seem a bit odd to include other P&C products in the cross-marketing, rather than the cross-selling or sales management sections, but we have done this for a reason. If your retail operation has not been in the habit of selling products from certain sectors of the P&C business, then we believe that treating these opportunities as entirely new undertakings makes sense. These product groups such can grow into sub-specialties or even departments within your retailing operation; alternatively, some or all of them can be referred outside to specialists, perhaps in the "wholesale" part of the marketplace.

Indeed, some P&C product groups require special expertise and a customized sales approach of their own. Here are some of the P&C "specialties" that might fall in this category, with a few notes about each.

Employment Practices Liability Insurance

First introduced in the early 1980s as an endorsement to some large D&O policies, employment practices liability (EPL) insurance has gradually grown in acceptance and importance. By the early 1990s, coverage was available on a standalone basis from approximately ten different markets; that number has increased to over twenty-five sources now. Additionally, a number of standard-lines carriers began offering EPL protection as an endorsement or adjunct coverage to their commercial lines policies.

EPL contracts protect the insured employer against charges of discrimination based on age, sex, or race in hiring, evaluating, promoting, and firing, against sexual harassment and wrongful discipline complaints, and often against a variety of other allegations involving various local, state, and federal standards (including EEOC investigations, the Americans With Disabilities Act (ADA), etc.). In many Federal District Courts in the late 1990s, employment-related claims made up more than half the pending case load. Suits and claims, both valid and spurious, continue to increase in frequency. Defense costs can quickly mount beyond five figures. Settlements and successful claims are not at all unusual and frequently involve large sums as well. Obviously, insurance retailers can do their clients a real service by explaining and offering EPL protection to them.

Oddly enough, EPL products have not been sold at nearly the pace expected or hoped for by the underwriting companies. This means that the product can be used as a real "door opener" for organizations that elect to learn enough about the product and the human resources (HR) support systems that accompany it. As with all lines of insurance, EPL is best deployed in combination with loss prevention and loss control measures. In fact, most EPL underwriters require certain procedural standards in the HR area before coverage is offered — things like an acceptable "Application for Employment," a written policy on the handling of sexual harassment complaints, an employment manual with requisite wording, and perhaps other internal procedures.

Note here, with an EPL sale, how the insurance retailer has suddenly gotten involved in a very different type of relationship with the client. The agent has the opportunity (or responsibility) to provide consultation (or at least access to expertise) on the running of the client's business. The retailer has now, to a greater extent than ever before, become a de facto member of the customer's management team. It is this new "twist" on the relationship which has probably kept P&C shops from selling a lot of EPL business — which requires a real re-thinking of the sales relationship. However, this is exactly the direction that you should be moving — toward becoming more and more valuable to the client and contributing directly to their profit and success.

International Insurance Coverages

More businesses every day expand into the field of international commerce. As trade barriers fall and as opportunities for growth spring up, the worldwide economy will penetrate virtually every business in the United States. You may assume that a certain commercial customer has no overseas activities, and you very well may be wrong.

Because most foreign countries are far less litigious than we are, coverage for exposures abroad can be surprisingly inexpensive. As of late 1997, at least three major carriers (AIG, Chubb, and CIGNA) had established full-blown international insurance and support capabilities. All three offer some variation of an "exporter's package policy" which can be delivered for a minimum premium as low as $2000.

A typical "exporters's package," for a small or medium-sized business that does some traveling abroad and has some sales abroad, typically contains (at a minimum) foreign general liability, excess foreign auto liability, and voluntary workers compensation (which will pay state-of-origin benefits for 24 injuries and for "endemic disease") that includes repatriation expense coverage (that gets the impaired employee or the remains back home). Where exposures exist, property and marine coverages can be included for things like sales samples, portable computers, and property in transit.

The major international carriers also have claim and service offices in many locations abroad, as well as corresponding relationships with "admitted" carriers in foreign markets to expedite placement of locally-required coverage (like for owned autos overseas, or property coverage for plants, warehouses, or offices abroad). Coverage can easily be customized for any conceivable combination of domestic and international insurance exposures, using combinations of admitted, non-admitted and differences in conditions (DIC) property and liability forms. These carriers can also offer special services such as travel warnings, travel tips, local toll-free emergency assistance, and the like.

Access to any of these international specialty markets is not difficult to obtain. CIGNA International and AIG usually operate on an "open brokerage" arrangement, and accept submissions from most retailers without a contract. Even Chubb can often be accessed through E&S wholesaling shops. Here again, your producers do not need to learn everything about the field of international insurance in order to help your customers with these needs. They only need to remember to ask about possible exposures, and to know that expert help (from the underwriting companies themselves, in this case) is just a phone call away. You might ask one of the underwriters from a nearby regional office of an international specialist insurer to make a two-hour presentation at your next sales meeting — they'd be delighted to, and your producers will then have enough knowledge to feel comfortable about bringing up the overseas questions with current clients. Then, even when a relatively tough international challenge comes up (say, the need for kidnap & ransom coverage for executives), your people will know who to call to get started.

Given the rapid expansion of international trade, some retailers are developing a specialty in this type of protection, and are using this knowledge as their door opener for a lot of new business. The larger regional and national brokers have used this strategy for a long time — reacting in mock horror when they "discover" that the local agent writing the account hasn't talked to them about the need for worldwide protection. You can be certain that if your people don't ask about these needs, it will be only a short time before someone else does — and you will have lost another fine account.

Directors & Officers (D&O) Liability and Other "Executive" Coverages

All but the smallest of a retailer's corporate clients are solid prospects for D&O insurance proposals. This is as true for not-for-profit (NFP) corporations as it is for publicly-traded manufacturers. Particularly where there are "outside" directors (and usually all the directors at NFP corporations are "outside"), there will be sensitivity to liability exposures inherent in these roles. In the United States, directors may be sued as individuals for a variety of real or imagined mistakes, by customers, competitors, regulators, business neighbors, employees and others. Yes, corporate bylaws often provide for "company reimbursement" of financial losses suffered by their directors in such situations, but this doesn't eliminate the problem: the corporation may not have adequate resources to defend or reimburse losses, and even if they do the losses could be very damaging to their operation.

Once again, the primary habit to inculcate in the retailer's staff is to ask, and to know enough about the exposures and the coverages to bring the nature of the risk more fully to the awareness of the client. They don't have to be full-blown experts on D&O protection. Once interest is aroused, the responsibility of the retailer's managers is to have in place two or three relationships with D&O experts, ready to provide advice and assistance for your producers.

If "qualified plans" (pensions, etc.) are in place at a customer's business, Trustees must be appointed. These trustees, under ERISA legislation, can be held personally liable for certain types of mismanagement, mistakes, or losses to the plan. Trustees and Fiduciaries Liability (TFL) is the solution here, and it is often an easy sale. A situation like this is ideal for a "team" approach involving both the L&H and the P&C specialists. If your shop sells pension plans, etc., have you called on every one of them to suggest TFL?

With your most valuable, fastest-growing commercial customers, you certainly want to have positioned your organization as helpful in D&O and related areas before that customer makes a major acquisition or "goes public." Why? Because regional and national brokers have an intelligence network that identifies every such transaction or filing very early in the process. Their next step is to stop in at your customer and say, "It's a whole new ballgame. Your local agent did a fine job when your operation was small, but now you need the kinds of help that only we can bring to the table." Your consistent objective should be to have your customer so well-protected and well-served that they just laugh at the "big boys" when they make this pitch.

Miscellaneous Professional Liability ("E&O")

There are literally hundreds of classes of business that present themselves as having special, "professional" skill and knowledge. The customers of those businesses (and the Courts) likewise will hold them to the "professional" standards and results implicit in the business relationship. If you think your commercial customer doesn't have these exposures, take another look. E&O coverage today is sold not only to physicians, attorneys, accountants, and engineers, but also to businesses as far-ranging as interior decorators, travel agents, ad agencies, printers, athletic trainers, crop seed sellers, consultants, computer software firms, and many others. Train your people to recognize these possible exposures, ask probing questions that will bring the customer's "worry" up to the level it should be, and to get access to the appropriate wholesaler or underwriter specialists for a proposal.

The critical concept to keep in mind with all these "specialty" P&C coverages is that, although you may not be comfortable working with these coverages now, you and your co-workers must learn enough about them to become so. Otherwise, sooner or later, you will be faced with an E&O claim because you should have recommended and provided the coverage. In other cases, you may lose some of your best customers to competitors who start talking about some of these "obvious" gaps in your protection program. It is both your responsibility and your opportunity to identify these client exposures, when they exist, and to provide your clients with access to the corresponding protection and service they require in these areas. These solutions may be handled in-house as your producing force gains the comfort level and the expertise required to present these issues. Until that time, you can provide an efficient conduit to the appropriate specialty markets for your clients.

"Un-bundling" the Insurance Product

As insurance retailers work with larger commercial clients and prospects, challenges and opportunities will arise that require the breaking up of the traditional insurance product. Often, these situations also involve insurance market "alternatives," which are discussed in the next section. In the context of the cross-marketing discussion, we suggest here again that you have at least someone on staff or "on call" who is conversant with these approaches. A periodic review of your larger accounts by this person would then be in order. The objective here is to stay a half-step ahead of your best customer's needs, anticipating them and discussing them a bit before they need addressing. Not-coincidentally, this half-step lead will also keep you ahead of potential competitors who might otherwise woo your clients with talk of a "new approach."

Claims Management

Reviewing claims and paying valid ones is a major component of the "financial transaction" side of the insurance product (see "Leveraging the

Redefined Insurance Product" at the beginning of Chapter 3). This activity has historically been undertaken by the underwriting insurance company providing the coverage (or their appointed "independent adjuster"). Today, though, such processes are frequently handled by insureds (in self-insured situations) or by third party administrators (TPAs). Some larger agencies have incorporated TPA activities into their suite of offered services, while others have farmed these activities out to professional TPA organizations. TPA activity is even more widespread on the group health side: almost all self-funded and partially self-funded groups have medical, disability income, and life claims handled through such arrangements.

If your shop services or calls on accounts large enough to need TPA services now or in the future, it would be time well spent to search for and become familiar with a select group with offices in your region. Lay the groundwork for these relationships now, so that they can be activated on short notice.

Loss Control

As insurance companies go through "downsizing" and "re-engineering," and as the soft market continues to curtail available dollars, many companies have cut back on the extent and the quality of ancillary services they provide to insureds, including loss control engineering. The need for these services has not disappeared, but they may not be available, or available to the extent needed. This situation presents additional revenue options to the savvy insurance retailer. Explain to your insured that 70% or more of most insurance dollars still go to pay claims, and that the route to continued long-term savings, soft market or not, is to maintain a pristine loss record. Then, offer to provide expert loss control services (for a fee), and use your own in-house expert or refer the business to a loss control firm with whom you have an arrangement.

An approach to controlling client loss frequency and severity being explored by a few progressive agencies is to help with business management, processes and procedures. This approach gets the retailer even more closely involved in the client's planning and operations; if done well, the agent becomes virtually invulnerable to competitive threats. Better management and internal processes can and do translate directly into fewer and less severe losses. If these advantages can be communicated to underwriters, then insurance premium savings, beyond those that would be available otherwise, can often be obtained. For more on ways to help your customers with the business of running their business, see "Cross-Marketing Non-Insurance Products and Services," on page 125.

Insurance Market "Alternatives"

In addition to the "un-bundling" of insurance policies with respect to claims and loss control, there are alternative ways of handling the "risk financing" component of the insurance transaction. Under these arrangements, rather than relying directly upon an underwriting insurance company to pay losses when they happen, losses are funded internally (through some form of self-insurance or captive arrangement) and/or with the professional reinsurance markets (either directly, or through a risk retention group, pool, or association). These approaches are arranged primarily to reduce the cost of risk, by disintermediating the insurance company (and sometimes, removing the agent from the picture as well). By removing one or more "layers" from the insurance transaction, costs can be lowered, and more dollars are available to pay for those claims that do happen.

The alternative market is estimated to cover 40% of U.S. commercial insurance exposures in the late 1990s (and even more, if the retained losses involved in high deductible and retrospectively rated plans are included). Perhaps partly because of the prolonged softening of the traditional market since the mid-1980s, the alternatives' percentage of the market has not grown significantly in the most recent years. At the same time, though, because the economy is constantly growing, many more individual accounts have migrated to alternatives.

This migration presents both a threat, and an opportunity, to the insurance retailer. In situations where a commercial account converts all or part of their insurance program over to an alternative approach, the servicing agent's revenue will fall off considerably. The opportunity lies in whether the agent can remain in the picture at all. If, through providing guidance, expertise, and various services, the retailer can assist in the administration, program design, and placement of reinsurance and unbundled services, then the retailer's competitive position is virtually unassailable. Keep in mind that migration back from the alternative market to traditional insurance is extremely rare. By helping to guide your client down this "one way street," an agent will find that the relationship can still be very profitable. Often, such assistance is compensated on a fee basis, rather than through commissions; it is much easier to predict business profits from fees than from soft-market commission arrangements.

For those retailers who climb the rather steep "alternative market" learning curve in order to hang on to a growing, valuable account, there can be "spillover" advantages. These arise from the fact that you have now worked with alternatives before and that you are the local "expert" in this area. Being able to intelligently talk about real alternatives and cost savings with prospects can be an extremely effective door opener to new business. Many agencies have had alternative market changes forced upon them, only to turn around and sell their newly acquired expertise in a broader, exciting marketplace.

A Word On Captives

For the most part, retailer involvement in captive insurance company arrangements will be confined to so-called "rent-a-captives," whereby the client gains direct access to reinsurance markets using the springboard of an already-established captive facility. Full captives, or single-parent captives, remain the province of the very largest corporations; at times, national or regional brokers will provide captive management or other services to such full captives, but these activities are at a level beyond those to which most smaller retailers can aspire. On the other hand, the possibility of facilitating a rent-a-captive solution to one or more of your larger clients is entirely possible.

Such an arrangement follows a pattern that by now the reader should be getting very familiar with: learn enough about the solution to be able to ask potential prospects about related problems. If the problems exist and the rough outline of the solution sparks interest, then hand off the actual implementation to full-time professionals with whom you retain a relationship.

Several sources exist for "full-time, professional" expertise in arranging rent-a-captive programs. We're most familiar with what is probably the largest true "turnkey" provider of such programs, Mutual Risk Management "MRM" (an NYSE-traded public company domiciled in Philadelphia). Through their Commonwealth Risk Services, Inc. subsidiary (which works only with agents and brokers), they can respond quickly and flexibly to a variety of scenarios. The Mutual Risk family includes Legion Insurance Company (highly-rated, and admitted in all states), MRM Hancock Ltd (a London reinsurance broker), Park International (providing wholesale access to the excess catastrophe market in Bermuda), Legion Management Corporation (with access to over 80 TPAs), The Worksafe Group, Inc. (for loss control activities), and Mutual

Indemnity, Ltd. (at the time of this writing, the only captive company rated A- by A.M. Best in 1997), and a variety of other captive and captive managment facilities in various domiciles. The MRM people can and do structure a variety of programs, including agency-owned captives, homogenous and non-homogenous group and association captives, and others.

When a possible prospect for a rent-a-captive or other solution arises, we encourage the retailer to investigate more than one source for possible solutions. Ask your major carriers, your wholesalers, and other agencies who they would suggest you contact with an alternative market proposal. Then contact two or three, tell them what you have in mind, and get proposals from the one or two that seem most responsive.

Cross-Marketing Non-Insurance Products and Services

Cross-marketing arises naturally from the selling process itself. As we saw in the Introduction, the best salespeople deploy one variety or another of what Neil Rackham calls "SPIN" selling, asking questions about the prospect's or client's **S**ituation, focusing in on **P**roblems that exist, probing further to heighten the buyer's awareness of the **I**mplications of those problems, and further refining the discussion to lay bare real **N**eeds. In addition to Rackham's classic *SPIN Selling*, we also recommend the follow-up published in 1996, *The SPIN Selling Fieldbook: Practical Tools, Methods, Exercises, and Resources*.

Yes, it would be a less painful world if the only problems were insurance problems; and yes, your salesperson's day would go much better if every prospect had lots of insurance problems. Sad to say, though, people and businesses have all kinds of problems. Unfortunately, most of them don't have serious insurance problems at the time your salespeople happen to be calling on them. What to do?

Logically, if there is no insurance problem, there will be no insurance sale. Nevertheless, you have already invested significant time and money to identify, research, and begin building a relationship with this prospect, as well as to deploy your sales talent to the prospect's office. The typical producer reaction to these situations in the past has been to fall back and say, "Well, there may not be anything significantly wrong with your current insurance program, but we can probably do the same thing for you a lot cheaper — why not let us give you a quote." Such an approach to our core business is nonsensical. We're talking about selling insurance here, not microprocessors. Moore's Law (the observation that the number of transistors on a chip doubles every eighteen months) does not apply to insurance policies. If your people and your competition keep selling insurance cheaper, in cycle after cycle, after a while either your agency or the companies you represent (or both) will be bankrupt.

It's much better to walk away from such a sales call and find another prospect, one that really needs what you're selling. It would be better yet to respond by attempting to satisfy the prospect's (or customer's) *non-insurance needs*. Of course, you'll eventually want to pick up as much of the insurance program as you can, and that will be relatively easy to do, once you have proven your worth in other areas. What other areas? We'll mention a few possibilities later, but these are as much to get the reader thinking about possibilities as they are to provide specific guidance.

This is the point where the insurance sales organization that is already taking advantage of cross-selling opportunities, actually *crosses the line* — into a much broader definition of its purpose and into a much better appreciation of its potential. Your prospect has no insurance problems today? That's OK, just proceed to ask about his or her other business concerns or issues that are challenging or troubling; then, when one comes up that you can help with, a personal connection is developed. At that point a sale can be made and the sales relationship truly begins.

Let's suppose that your agency has already established contacts with strong, service-oriented providers in the fields of lending, business planning, and international commerce law. You don't have these experts on your payroll, but you do have arrangements whereby they will respond immediately to the "leads" your people provide them. Furthermore, since they don't have to go through the trouble and expense required to prospect and build these relationships themselves, they are more than willing to share any corresponding revenues with you in the form of a "finders fee" or commission. Your customer is happy (you've solved his or her problem), you are happy (you've made some money from the sales call), and the corresponding vendor is happy (they got a red-carpet introduction to a client they probably would not have known about). A *win-win-win* situation.

As a competitive tool, cross-marketing is every bit as effective and important with your current clients as it is with prospects. Insurance customers are likely to ask, "What have you done for me lately?" The only long-term defense you have against outside competition is for your organization to be extremely valuable, make that *indispensible*, to your customers. If, in addition to a providing a great insurance program, you have also helped finance an expansion, helped streamline their distribution system, and put them in touch with a big new opportunity — then, and only then, will you be though of as indispensible.

Cross-marketing starts when you establish contacts with top-rung service providers in a variety of fields. It progresses as you regularly ask clients and prospects about a broad range of problems and reaches full fruition only when it becomes a way of doing business, a state of mind that has your organization providing access to a wide variety of business and personal solutions for your clients. Now let's take a look at a few potential fields that could be used as a starting point for this transformation.

Business Consulting

There are consultants in almost every area of expertise imaginable today, but only a handful have all the business they would like. To address this need most insurance retailers should be spending a portion of their time identifying and cultivating vending relationships with consultants in a variety of specialties such as computer networking, exporting, telecommunications, ISO 9000 certification, business planning, advertising, legal subspecialties, and the like. Then, make your salespeople aware that your organization can provide easy access to these consultants when their prospects or clients have a related problem or need. In order to make just the right "connection" they may need to ask a few more pointed questions, perhaps probing in a some new directions.

For example, suppose a producer is reviewing the P&C insurance program for mid-size client a few weeks ahead of policy renewals. In asking about business personal property limits for the coming year, the client mentions they have budgeted $350,000 for developing an "intranet" to connect their eight locations with their customers. Our savvy and well-prepared producer then asks, "Oh? Who's going to integrate that system with your current database?" The client replies that they will be sending out RFPs (Requests for Proposals) in a couple of weeks. The producer then asks if they have considered talking to the folks at "Net-Wurx," a consultant that your agency has identified as being a leader in the state at just this sort of thing. The producer knows just enough about what "Net-Wurx" does and about their reputation to get your client interested. You then set up the appointment and make an introduction. If "Net-Wurx" gets the contract, your agency gets a commission for the introduction.

Don't think that you have to have answers for every conceivable problem. Instead, just get started with one or two businesses or professionals that you have already worked with. You may even be able to start off by promoting the services of one of your existing clients — which is a great way of significantly improving several of your business relationships at once!

Access to Capital and Lending Markets

What one thing does virtually every business need? Money, and more money; lots of money; cheap money. If your agency has established relationships with money sources, and can bring them to bear when your clients and prospects are in need, you and your producers will be heroes. While there has been a long, often dramatic, discussion about the disruptive nature of "banks in insurance," we predict that a much greater impact will result from the growth of "insurance in banking." Commercial P&C operations have a much more solid relationship with most of their clients than do most commercial banks. Our producers visit the client more often and have more relationships (and friendships) with our clients and their employees than do commercial lenders. We know more about our customers' businesses than the banks do. We can sell — selling is our core competency, our business roots are in selling, selling is our lifeblood. The roots of banking are in taking deposits and cautiously considering loan applications.

Banks have made various forays into insurance retailing in recent years, with varying degrees of success (or lack thereof). Many have found out just how tough the insurance retailing business is, and have backed off or scaled down their plans for insurance activities. Enticed by the same "cross-marketing" principles that we're discussing here, banks wish to earn more revenue per customer and hope at the same time to solidify their relationship with these customers.

A very steep learning curve confronts banks and other financial institutions that want to sell insurance — they must learn all about insurance, and they must also learn how to sell. As we have already seen, though, effective insurance selling requires more than just technical sales knowhow; it also requires a knowledge of the underlying sales culture and a true sales organization infrastructure. We know of more than one bank that has balked at commercial P&C (or Life and Benefits) selling when it became clear that top producers could (and should) earn considerably more than bank Division Vice

Presidents — an almost intolerable state of affairs. Some respond by paying their producers less — so their good producers leave them, and those without energy or sales talent remain.

Banks are discovering another way of meeting these goals (i.e., increasing revenues per customer, gaining more customers, and strengthening relationships with customers to keep competition at bay) — and this is to establish any of a variety of joint venture or partnership arrangements with existing insurance retailers. Especially in commercial lines of insurance, banks are finding it much easier (and more profitable) to "exchange" or "cross-refer" customers with a good insurance agency than it would be to buy and try to run that agency or to start up a competitive operation from scratch. In one scenario, the bank introduces its commercial loan clients to the local insurance agency in a formal, face-to-face meeting. The agency then begins the insurance selling process, and if successful, pays part of the revenues from that account to the bank. Reciprocity arises when the insurance agency brings their insurance clients to the bank, again with a formal introduction, suggesting that they consider doing their commercial banking with the correspondent bank.

Establishing a relationship like this with one or more area banks could make a lot of sense for many insurance retailers. However, other options also exist and there certainly will be many new permutations on this basic idea. For instance, we know of one organization with a lot of experience in the financial world that serves as a clearing house for all kinds of transactions — including equipment leasing, accounts receivable financing, venture capital, bankruptcy financing, expansion loans, and many others. This organization markets its services through insurance agencies, who receive attractive fees for bringing in business. This organization not only provides access to money markets, but also helps clients prepare business plans or loan applications in a manner that makes them attractive to the lenders.

By providing access to these resources and ancillary services, your agency becomes a key part of the success and growth of your clients' businesses. Instead of being perceived as merely another expense item on their financial statement ("insurance premiums"), you can transform your client's perception so that you are seen as a reliable provider of income, resources, and growth. This type of recognition is significant, and will keep your now-loyal commercial customers from even talking with your insurance competition.

Employee Leasing and Human Resources Outsourcing Opportunities

A revolution is underway in the way American businesses engage human resources. The traditional employer-employee relationship has splintered into a variety of approaches to the need for work and talent. These alternatives include outsourcing, business process redesign (and attendant "re-engineering"), leasing of employees (through co-employment relationships with professional employment organizations or PEOs), and a variety of "partnering" arrangements with suppliers, customers, and occasionally even competitors. Sales opportunities for the insurance retailer exist in this area as well.

The principles involved are the same as those in other types of cross-marketing activities — by now they should be familiar: identify top-quality service providers, establish relationships with them in which you agree to do some of their prospecting for them, educate your producers about the availability of these resources and train them to be on the lookout for client or prospect needs that would indicate an openness to help from your contacts.

There are hundreds of PEO service organizations that provide workers compensation, employee benefits, HR administration, or payroll services. The client retains all hiring, firing, and disciplinary responsibilities. In this way, a "joint employment," or "co-employer," relationship is formed. While PEOs (formerly known as employee leasing companies) have had a somewhat checkered past, they have gained respectability and credibility in the business community. For many businesses, the promise of better benefits at lower cost, combined with the freedom from keeping up with all the regulatory changes and paperwork required in an HR department, make the PEO option an attractive one.

Often, insurance retailers first become aware of the PEO industry when a commercial customer calls them in to announce they are moving their workers compensation and group insurance programs away from the agent, as part of their move to a PEO. This business, once gone, is unlikely ever to return to the agency. To compound the problem, many PEOs have arrangements with insurance agencies who themselves get an introduction and recommendation by the PEO to the PEO's new client. There are a few important endorsements that should be made to the client's liability and other insurance coverages that result from this joint employment relationship — this is a natural "door opener" for the new competition to start taking the rest of the account away.

A couple of tactics suggest themselves here. First, why not locate a respected, growing PEO and offer to introduce them to your clients? It would not be unusual for the commission from such a sale to be quite a bit larger than those arising out of the whole P&C and Group insurance program. Second, if your timing is right, you might get the opportunity to be the provider of workers compensation and/or group benefits to all of the PEO's clients. Pursuing either of these options requires a bit of study, research, and planning, but the rewards can be considerable.

Although employee leasing is a growing industry, most employers continue to find that step a little too radical. For such businesses, whether current clients or prospects, it would behoove the insurance retailer to develop access to less drastic options that will help administer HR activities. There are numerous HR data management, talent search firms, legal specialists, payroll processing companies and similar service organizations in every state. Some are clearly better than others; some can offer a very broad suite of consulting and outsourced services. Why not call on a few in your area? Talk to them about the possibility of having your sales staff send some business their way, for a fee.

In this area, as in many others, attention must be given to contract details; a critical matter is determining just who "owns" the customer. If you are unhappy with the service being provided, can you just move the business to another firm? Obviously, this arrangement is preferable to one in which you are constrained from providing alternate choices in the future. For many situations, a "new and renewal" payment arrangement is worth negotiating for — it keeps the revenues coming in to your organization and keeps you in touch with your client in these expanding fields of activity.

Keeping up-to-date with your clients' current business concerns and plans for the future (which is necessary anyway to do a good job on their insurance program) will give you an advantage in suggesting and selling a variety of valuable business services. To start, your role may be as simple as recommending a vendor whom you know and trust, one who can help your client cut or control costs. By regularly asking clients about the vendors they use for certain services and noting the names of those they give "rave reviews," you will have identified potentially valuable sources of new business. Contacting that vendor with a new piece of business (i.e., your client) may pay off in several ways, including making that firm a potential insurance customer.

There are many business services that you could easily learn enough about to "sell" your clients and prospects on. Of course there will always be new products and services arising from the creative work of a variety of industries that incorporate innovative new approaches to business problems. One thing these new developments will all have in common, however, will be that their creators will be anxious to find some way of getting the "word" out; they'll be looking for someone to sell their ideas — preferably someone who already has an "in" with their targeted prospects. That someone might as well be you.

"Client-Centric" Marketing

In the old days, L&H and P&C companies viewed themselves as product providers. They would create property and casualty and/or life insurance products designed to meet certain broad, general market needs, and then would recruit and train agents with those products in mind. These agents had to be able to identify and sell to those prospects who had the "right" needs, those for whom the company's products were designed.

Under this "product- or process-centric" strategy, companies sold what they had to sell and consumers bought what was offered (or went without). As companies have attempted to broaden their product offerings, they've tried to broaden their agents' training to sell an ever-widening range of products. At a certain stage of growth in product numbers and variety, though, another approach to marketing has arisen, for the most part outside the awareness of the companies. Without understanding where they were going, they were actually making possible a shift to a "client-centric" sales strategy.

The "client-centric" strategy places the client at the very center of the business universe, attempts to recognize that client's specific, individual needs, and then finds a way to provide tailored solutions.

Some financial services companies and insurance retailers have awakened to the realization that a customer can be retained once an initial level of trust is established. This trust arises out of an explicit orientation of the company toward that customer's set of needs as they change over time. This long-term relationship has another societal trend reinforcing it — the frenetic pace of the world today. Most of the most valuable customers have multiple, overlapping, demands competing for their time — family, business, education, and recreation to name a few. These demands leave consumers with even less time to deal with the critically important, but "put-off-able," items like buying life insurance, doing wills, estate planning, long-term care, and just thinking about the future in general.

The successful client-centric marketer will find time efficient ways to interface with the customer that are convenient *for the customer*. By doing business this way, the marketer is in fact meeting just another need—the need for more time. It's just too time intensive for your customers to go through all the groundwork, teaching your competitor about their likes, dislikes, plans, and lifestyle. With this added marketing advantage you're likely to get a positive and prompt response when you have a new product or service to sell.

Of course, the time savings must be *real* and noticeable to your customer. Your service and advice must be prompt, professional, and accurate. Your customer must also come to believe that your products and services are priced at a fairly competitive level (many won't care if you're not always the cheapest, as long as you're easiest). Now, here's the rub. The existing agency sales force, on both the life and P&C sides, has been recruited and trained in a "product-centric" rather than a "client-centric" mode. All of your people will have to develop the new skill sets and outlook that are required to succeed with this new sales strategy.

At State Farm Insurance, one of the more successful companies at cross-selling training, this trend has been clearly recognized. According to Chuck Wright, Senior Vice President for Marketing and Agency Development, their agent of the future will be "managing relationships with customers." Since it would be unreasonable to assume most agents can become expert in all lines of insurance, it must be the company's job to supply access to and basic training in those areas outside the agents area of expertise. It's no surprise then that State Farm has made one of the strongest commitments in the industry to continuing education. In fact, on an annual basis, there are more CPCU, CLU, and ChFC designees from State Farm than from any other company.

Also, according to Mr. Wright, some producers will make the transition into relationship management well, and some will continue as they have been with a certain amount of success well out into the future. He sees no reason not to continue to support them and, where necessary, build the future around them. A lot of the future growth, however, will come through a younger, more technologically-sophisticated breed of agent who will be readily able to recognize, adapt to, and take advantage of changes in insurance buying patterns.

Whether selling insurance or solving other business or lifestyle problems, insurance retailers of the future must fix their focus on what the customer needs, and find a way to deliver solutions that are attractive, valuable, convenient, and cost-effective for their clients. A lot of their ability to satisfy those needs will come from the effective implementation of current and future communication and technology tools.

Chapter 7

Nurturing Sales Relationships with Technology and Communication

To say that electronic and communications technology are rapidly changing today's business environment is to state the obvious. The obvious, however, can sometimes mask more subtle implications. Rapid, ceaseless change often has the troublesome effect of numbing our sensibilities, interfering with our ability to sort it all out, even damping our will to keep up with it. In business, more than in any other field, the future will belong to those who can best deploy the tools of the day. In selecting and utilizing the tools of the future, it will be more important than ever to "keep an eye on the (sales) ball" — by weighing technology choices and strategies in the light of how they will support, or improve, the sales relationship.

Computers and related equipment can be a great help when thoughtfully integrated into a sales organization. A great agency recognizes the "time value of time" and accordingly finds every way possible to maximize the time producers are meeting face-to-face or "phone-to-phone" with their clients. Use of automated dialing systems, voicemail, and well-designed telemarketing systems are but a few examples of how successful retailers are translating "time into money." Color printers, fax machines, cellular communications, presentation software, contact managers, personal information managers — the list of tools that can effectively support an agency's sales efforts is extensive and growing.

Sales Force Automation Systems

Technically, only the larger, more complex software systems are "officially" categorized as Sales Force Automation (SFA) tools. Such systems are often complicated and expensive and their full implementation usually requires the expertise of a computer consultant, whether in-house or out-sourced. There are a number of the same tasks, however, that can be implemented by the judicious use of simpler, more cost-effective tools.

Keeping track of contacts, prospects, and customers is one such task. Up to a certain level, this can be managed quite effectively using contact management software on stand alone or networked computers. At the time of writing, the three most popular and well-reviewed programs in this category are *ACT!*, *Ecco Gold*, and *Goldmine*. A busy insurance producer will find in a few short months that many hundreds of names and addresses (and considerable other information) can be entered into such databases, which then can be integrated with calendars, "to-do" lists, and note taking, letter-writing, and contact history capabilities. We have yet to talk with a user of contact management software who would even consider going back to the old, comparatively inefficient, manual (i.e. card-based) systems that preceded it. Business and personal life have just gotten too hectic and complex not to get automated help on at least this level.

A few of the better agency management software systems have built-in "marketing modules" that can at least be set up to run and keep track of various sales campaigns and programs. Effective selling requires relationship building, and the foundation for these relationships can efficiently be laid with the organized use of phone calls, letters, reminders, and mailers. To be effective, such marketing programs must be consistently coordinated, monitored, and updated. Implementing the marketing module in your existing agency management system could lend considerable order to these tasks.

An objective to keep in mind regarding agency automation planning is maintaining continuity in your interaction with prospects and customers. When this is achieved, your producers can continue a conversation right where the last interaction left off — even if the most recent person to speak with that customer was someone other than the original contact (who may now be "away from her desk," ill, on vacation, laid off, or dead). This objective can be difficult to achieve, but it is an important one. For example, if you utilize both a "contact management" program and a high-level "agency management" system, both have "history" and note-taking capabilities. Are you making sure that all interactions are logged consistently into both systems? Will the next person answering the phone have ready access to notes about the prior contact?

Most business and personal lines insurance customers expect their retailers to remember what they've been told. The electronic file on a customer or prospect should have in one place, all the basic information about them. One of the authors recently spoke with a business owner who was very displeased with his P&C agency: a new producer had been assigned to service his account, and this producer asked the insured what the relationship was among the three insureds on his liability coverage. "I don't care if he is a new employee," he said, "they're supposed to know that stuff. It should be in the file. Why should I have to explain it twice?" Why indeed.

At a more advanced level, true SFA tools come into play. Selecting such a system, particularly one that will effectively integrate with your other agency systems, should be a priority project involving a great deal of research and planning. Here, the use of both outside consultants and the Internet would be a good starting point. Using your favorite search engine, search on the phrase "Sales Force Automation" — and be prepared to wade through dozens of options.

All of these tools should be focused on a few specific outcomes — finding more prospects, establishing credible contacts with them, explaining what your business is and does for potential customers, keeping sales campaigns on track, and giving your producers more time to spend in face-to-face production situations.

Expert Systems and "Just-in-time" Training

With the processing power (or price/performance ratios) of computer systems doubling every eighteen months or so, what seemed like mad speculation a few years ago is commonplace today. Let's jump ahead just a couple of processor "generations" and speculate on what to expect over the next three to five years when computers will be four to eight times more powerful than they are today. Actually, the systems we'll discuss here could be put in place today, with today's technology — it would just wouldn't be cost effective to do so. Certainly, a number of software and insurance industry groups are already developing the major components of this or a similar "system of the future," or have envisioned something every bit as radical.

Recall that the P&C retailer adds value to the insurance transaction in large part by being positioned to know first-hand about the client's situation and by being trusted to answer the client's important questions. Add to this recollection the most constraining force on any retailer's growth: the lack of actual selling time available for experienced, talented producers. Consider, then, what would happen if we could provide energetic, but inexperienced producers with a "backup" — an expert-in-a-box, if you will.

In a few short years, we can imagine the apprentice or journeyman producer calling on a complex commercial prospect carrying a small notebook-sized appliance. Set unobtrusively to the side (no typing in this sales call!), the producer begins, after a pleasantry or two, asking a couple of questions about the situation and problems at the prospect's business. These aren't dumb questions, though, because the agency's research staff has already learned a lot about the prospect's business, plans, resources, products, size, and industry. These are "smart" questions, designed by the artificial intelligence engines in the notebook to uncover those areas where the agency is most likely to be able to offer assistance.

The notebook works primarily with speech recognition, distinguishes the producer's voice from the prospect's, and provides teleprompter-like cues for the producer to probe further into areas with potential. Imagine that this conversation gets side-tracked a little when the prospect asks a tough, obscure, subtle question whose answer requires a great deal of experience and communication skill. The producer then simply suggests that they bring a specialist in to the conversation; at this point, the notebook establishes a cellular or satellite video and audioconferencing session with a "back office" specialist. Perhaps a number of agencies around the state have pooled their "old hands" together so that several are available at any time during business hours, and a few are available on-call 24 hours a day, 365 days a year — to lend a guiding hand to the novices out in the field.

This "expert in a box" would have instant access to the needed data and background, to be able to answer the question in context. There might be a suggestion that the producer first run the DVD (digital video disk) segment in the notebook's library to define and illustrate a couple of the terms under discussion, and then run a short, animated presentation illustrating the most subtle points (which is downloaded as needed to the notebook in the field by the expert in the back office).

Such a system would walk the producer and prospect in an orderly, comprehensive manner, as far along in the sales process as they wished to go that day. Certain facts and details gained in the interview would automatically trigger the asking of questions in related areas. For instance, if it turns out the client is engaged in exporting and importing, a series of questions that lead to the underwriting and pricing of appropriate international insurance coverages are automatically asked (or bookmarked for later review).

At the end of a half day's visit, the producer will be able to present, without ever leaving the prospect's office, a formal proposal, even experimenting with a number of optional retention and coverage options to tweak the proposal into optimal form. The prospect agrees to the proposal and the producer uploads the policy contract language onto the new client's network, activates an EFT (electronic transfer of funds) relay to pay the premiums, and both parties are comforted to know that the system will automatically prompt enough contacts and questions so that everything in the insurance program keeps pace with any changes in client's business.

What we have described here is just one of the many possible interfaces of the system of the future. Using technology such as this, the smallest particular preferences that the insurance customer might express can be honored. "Let's just do this over the phone." Fine. "I like to work on stuff like this after midnight, on weekends." Not a problem. "Can I come to your place?" Of course. "Could we do this in a videoconference?" You bet. "When I have a question, I'll e-mail you, but I want a response within three hours, no matter what or when." Can do.

An additional benefit is that such a system for vending and servicing insurance protection could deliver that insurance at a much lower cost traditional insurance delivery methods. Why? For one reason, you might have noticed in the above scenario that there was no insurance company involved. The risk was automatically laid off to a worldwide, networked consortium of reinsurers and financial institutions, that are confident in the front-line underwriting powers of the system deployed.

Really, there wasn't a tremendous amount of insurance agency involvement in the scenario, either. If you selected ten agencies today at random, each with $1 to $2 million dollars of annual revenues, you would likely find that each one has on its staff at least one, and maybe two, highly-trained, technically skilled, seasoned and savvy producers. People with such skills and talents are expensive, but if you follow them around for a week, you will discover that on a visible level, they actually use this experience and talent only a small percentage of the time. The remainder of their time is spent in tasks of a lower order. Each shop needs these people to be "on call" in case a tough question or situation does come up.

Realistically, the ten agencies in question don't need a total of fifteen or twenty such people, though — four or five would probably do nicely, if their talent could get out in the field, on an as-needed basis. Tomorrow's marketplace will demand that efficiencies of this scale be achieved, and tomorrow's technology will make it possible.

The Internet

The attempt to explain the import and scope of the Internet in a few paragraphs would be as sophomoric as to write a three-page term paper on "The Universe" or "The History of the World." What might be said about it today, similarly, will fall far short of where it will be tomorrow. Just as we cannot educate a computer about what life is, we should not expect humans to understand the universe of the Internet by talking or reading about it. Dive in, use it, explore it, wade around in it, get pulled by its currents, experience it!

There is almost no aspect of business life that cannot be enhanced or deepened through the Internet: research, selling, communication, marketing, recruiting, training, prospecting, expanding, purchasing, outsourcing, consulting, accounting, and on, and on, and on. Familiarity with the tools, processes, and protocols of the Internet will be required for success in business in the very near future. Get access, give your people access, and use it to your advantage.

Members of "Generation X" and of the "Baby Boom Echo" that follow them do not have the same views of, or relationship with, technology that older citizens have. Maybe the people you talk with assert they could never do without a "real live insurance agent," but they are your customers (those who aren't, may have different opinions). The upcoming generations of consumers will be either indifferent, or predisposed to prefer an all-electronic (or mostly-electronic) transaction. Convenience and cost will outweigh other concerns for many of them. They trust computers and networks, and will have engaged in hundreds of commercial transactions on-line by the time they reach the age of 30. How will you sell to them? How will they find you?

In the future "who you are" as a business will be judged in a large part by how good your web page is. Think of it as your electronic "storefront." With that in mind, make sure your agency's Home Page on the World Wide Web is easy to find, attractive, interactive, and simple to navigate. Establish as many web links as possible with insurance organizations, your underwriting companies, your customers, and with service providers from other businesses that you cross-market with. Show your URL (internet address) on all your agency communications — business cards, signs, letterhead, and advertisements. Utilize a talented web page designer, first to get the basics right, and then to periodically update page design and content. Make it easy for web "surfers" to e-mail you directly from your web page. Once you are up and running, be sure to regularly monitor your web page and treat inquiries made on the web like you would as if they were made over the phone or in person. Good customer service is just as critical here as it is when dealing with a customer or prospect face-to-face.

The Newsletter

It may seem a bit odd to be discussing a newsletter in a chapter devoted to technology issues, but rolling out and maintaining a good newsletter interfaces with a number of technology issues and software products. For example, some use word processing or desktop publishing software to produce their newsletters. Some "publish" newsletter content simultaneously in mailings and on the web Home Page. Knowing who to send the newsletter to, when to start with a prospect, and when to stop with a former customer requires interfaces with databases and marketing systems. To make your newsletter attractive and meaningful, digital photos and scanned graphics can be included. With just a little extra work and some help from automation, newsletter issues can be more or less individualized, for different customers or customer groups.

A great newsletter is like a good cologne. When you don't wear any, nobody notices. When you wear a really good one, folks think and sometimes say, "Isn't that terrific!"

Your newsletter should have a broader effect than just to "keep the agency's name in front of your clients and prospects." After deploying a regular newsletter for a year or so, you should be able to connect numerous sales or important referred leads, that you've made as a direct result of it. Of course, improving your business name identification is a good secondary goal, but the constant writing, printing and mailing can be an expensive way to attain this. Picture your own stacks of "backed up" reading, and remember that your client or prospect has their own stack of reading to take care of and that long, technical articles on insurance are likely to get tossed immediately.

The biggest mistake agencies make in their use of a newsletter is in not being sure of the real purpose of the newsletter. This real purpose is to offer appealing, quick, easy reading that will appeal to the target audience as individuals. It should be graphically interesting, fun to read, and have practical relevance to your audience's current concerns. Personal risk management and techniques on how to keep your insurance costs down are popular subjects. Just because we're in the insurance field doesn't mean we have to send out boring newsletters.

One of the authors of this book used to send out the typical "Tax" newsletters to clients many years ago, but even accountant and attorney clients would typically remark that they missed or hadn't yet read the last issue. Ten years ago, he switched formats entirely, sending out a combination Health & Fitness newsletter together with an enclosed, personally-written cover letter with short thoughts on motivation, self-improvement, or even an occasional (interesting) insurance or tax news item. In stark contrast to the old format, this new approach has consistently brought in identifiable and significant sales and referrals.

It may be a year or two before you really begin reaping the benefits of a good newsletter. After the client receives the newsletter for awhile and learns that it's always interesting and packed with valuable information, the results will be cumulative. You'll really know you've arrived when you call to get in touch with the president of one of your commercial clients and his administrative assistant answers the phone and says, "Oh you're the one who sends us out that newsletter we love so much. I make copies of it and take it home for my family to read. Mr. Jones is in a meeting with someone but let me see if I can interrupt." This has happened to the author on several occasions. I've even had administrative assistants leave their current employment or have their boss die, and ask if they can be kept on the mailing list.

Today, with the Internet as a research resource and the relative ease of desktop publishing, there are thousands of persons who can put together an attractive newsletter. Paying someone to work with you to produce an attractive newsletter or to just help with your personal cover letter is very easy, and not too expensive. Here are a few suggested "rules":

- Find a theme that fits in with your agency. One top P&C agency we know does a terrific newsletter; a regular part of it is sports and baseball trivia. Their very creative author covers mainly tax and insurance topics but does it in a humorous, "case study" format.

- Keep all the articles short. Your goal is to help clients fight the biggest problem we all face today "information overload." Find relevant information, put it into as few words as possible, and make it interesting and understandable.

- Vary the topics. If you decide to send out a pre-done "insurance" newsletter (you just add your corporate logo and masthead), that can be OK, assuming its content is bright, interesting, and easy-to-read. But with each issue, add a separate cover letter which you write (or pay someone to write) and make sure it's really fun: your "Wisdom of the Month;" insurance comedy; famous dates in history, etc.

The Life Underwriting Process of the Future

Another factor favoring the expansion of P&C agencies into the life business is the ongoing streamlining and automation of the underwriting process. The rapid automation of the process is already providing "productivity increases" which favor P&C agencies with larger blocks of personal lines business (as well as those with programs for commercial lines "workplace" marketing).

Few life insurance agents were ever cut out to be good administrative types. And although as a generalization, P&C agents tend to be more organized and on the analytical side, most P&C producers are not familiar with, nor are comfortable with, the medical underwriting side of the life business. Now, thanks to new technologies, expert systems, and third-party providers (e.g. tele-direct interviewers and underwriters) the agent is being removed from the underwriting loop at amazing speed. With most carriers either working on new automated systems or with one already in place, this trend will continue to expand geometrically in the foreseeable future. What does this mean for the P&C agency of the future and for the cross-selling of life insurance products?

For smaller, relationship driven agencies, it could mean doubling or tripling their number of life sales without an increase in overhead expenses. The agent can, in many cases, make the sale to an existing client over the phone (especially where term insurance is all that's needed), take down some preliminary information which often can be keyed directly into the insurance company's policyholder database. This entry triggers a tele-direct underwriter and/or tele-interviewer to call the prospect and directly ask the pertinent medical, avocation, financial justification, and other relevant questions. Often by utilizing a trained underwriter or medical tele-interviewer, decisions can be made instantaneously, eliminating the need for an Attending Physician's Statement (i.e. medical records). This streamlining can save a lot of money for the company and earn a lot of money for the involved agent.

As the client is being interviewed on the phone, these answers are being digitally transmitted into the "Home Office" expert system, which either stores the data or tranfers it into an "artificial intelligence" underwriting system. On relatively "clean" cases, this could mean an instantaneous approval and a policy ready for delivery in 24 to 48 hours.

All of this is going to further help P&C agencies, who are already in more frequent contact with clients than their traditional life counterparts. By removing the more laborious involvement in the details of underwriting and policy issuance, P&C agents (and here we're not just talking about life specialists but also P&C producers themselves) will become more active on the "life" side.

New Sales Visions

If you were to describe the ideal salesperson, or recall your best sales experience as a buyer, it would certainly be nothing like the "high-pressure" used car salesman, or Woody Allen's description of a fate "worse than death...being locked up in a storm cellar for several days with a life insurance salesman." Instead, our ideal salesperson might look and sound like Jimmy Stewart or Robert Young, have the communication skills of Colin Powell, Oprah Winfrey, or John F. Kennedy and could inform you with the ring of credibility like Peter Jennings, Ted Koppel, or Walter Cronkite.

And during the sales process, this ideal, "composite," salesperson would:

- establish trust almost the minute you met them

- educate you on the product or service in a very friendly and courteous manner

- answer all your questions and deal with all your concerns in a way that you felt was straightforward and to the point

- ask you to buy and help you complete your purchase in a way that made you put pressure on yourself rather than the other way around.

The best salespeople can tell when a prospect is just procrastinating and is asking to be "closed" again, or when he or she is really saying, "I'm just not ready now; don't push me any more." The difference is that even when the person who was closed (and asked to buy 3 or 4 times) is asked if he or she had been sold, they will say "No, I bought! The salesperson just helped lead me through my questions."

Now the $64,000 Question: "Will there be automated sales systems in the future which will have most of the qualities of our ideal salesperson? Our answer is a definite "Yes." Many of tomorrow's insurance consumers will log onto an insurance Internet web site from the comfort and privacy of their home or office and enter into dialogue an "underwriting system." Part of this dialogue will be with a skilled, attractive "talking head" using videoconferencing and part of it will be asking and answering questions verbally using voice recognition or through the use of a keyboard or scanner. In particularly large or complex situations, a "real human being" may be deployed to develop a thorough understanding of the situation.

In most cases, though, the consumer will have the ability to ask any question on your product or the service, at any comprehension level, with no fear of being laughed at or talked down to. The answers will come back in a language and format customized for the individual. If these answers lead to other questions, the consumer can dig deeper, or ask that the information be sent back by another medium (e.g. mail, fax) or with examples or case studies.

The purchase of insurance protection or related services will be almost an afterthought: as easy as pushing a button on a telephone or just saying "Go ahead." The fulfillment process — for example, a policy issuance — will be instantaneous in many cases. In just moments, the application is approved, the bank account is debited, and a "policy" is downloaded and e-mailed to the customer's home or office computer. The consumer can then print it out if they want to and put it into a safety deposit box. Much of this kind of information retrieval and research is already taking place everyday as more and more people discover how easy it is to find information on the World Wide Web.

The natural reaction of today's insurance producer is to ask, "Will a human salesperson even be needed?" Again, our answer is affirmative, however, the insurance producer of tomorrow will function somewhat differently. The salesperson of the future will function like a skilled librarian, whose value is derived from knowing where to go to get the "best" information on a topic, the best solution to the problem, and how to consolidate the mass of information available into an intelligible synthesis. Such a producer will act as an "information filter," making it easy for information overloaded clients to get just enough background for them to feel comfortable making important purchase decisions. These producers will also help to verify and pass along the required information about the client's risks, needs and history "upstream" to the underwriters and service providers.

APPENDIX 1

Making Hardware and Software Buying Decisions

Technology purchase decisions can be daunting. We've often heard people complain how computer hardware, especially, is a "moving target;" they hesitate to buy something today, fearing it will be obsolete in a few months. This is definitely not the case. While it is true that in a few months your hardware will no longer be the *latest* model, if you buy wisely, it will have complete utility and functionality for five years or more.

What does "buy wisely" imply? Let's start with personal computers (PCs), then we'll add a couple of notes about servers:

- Purchase from a major vendor, such as IBM, Compaq, Dell, Gateway 2000, Micron, NEC, or Toshiba - one whose name has been frequently mentioned in the product reviews in the computer trade press (also available on the Internet) as "recommended" or an "Editors' Choice." Compare the ratings not only for performance, but also for reliability, technical support, and service policies.

- When you are ready to actually place the order and commit your money, buy the second or third most powerful Intel microprocessor that is shipping at that moment. For example, at the time of this writing machines are being shipped with 300 MHz Pentium II processors — but you'll save more than $200 per unit buying the 266 MHz processor — without any sacrifice in functionality or ability to handle tomorrow's software demands (in a real budget crunch, you might step down one more layer, in this example to a 233 MHz speed, to save another $200 per unit). Consider alternatives to Intel processors carefully, preferably only with the help of a trusted consultant.

- Don't try to second-guess how you may want to be using the systems three or four years from now. Most systems come bundled with a number of what may seem today to be marginal features (like sound capability and speakers, advanced graphics cards, etc.) — go ahead and buy the bundle. The idea is to keep from ever opening the box. Hardware upgrades are time consuming and expensive — so don't gamble with your future.

- Get the absolutely biggest and best monitor you can afford. For one of the authors buying 45 PCs in late 1994, that meant getting 17" (15.9" or viewable) screens then. Today it would be 19" or 20". You and your people will literally spend months of your life peering at these screens — do not skimp here!

- Storage memory and RAM are both cheap, and getting cheaper — spend the few extra dollars to get a lot of each.

- For several years, the above combination of features has run at just under $3000 per seat, including monitors and network interface cards. This price point should hold for the foreseeable future — you will get a whale of a system for under $3000 current dollars whenever you buy — one that will not be outgrown for five or more years.

When purchasing file servers or database servers, check first with the vendor of the agency management system you will be using or converting to. Some insist you follow their specifications. Once you've covered the basics here, though, get your consultant's help and buy as robust and redundant a system as you can afford. Backup power supplies, RAID data storage (hot-swappable), redundant network cards, fast bus speeds, etc. are just the starting point for consideration. Believe us when we say you don't want your server to go down.

Agency management software purchase decisions are difficult as well. Again, we suggest you do a good deal of research before making a commitment. The insurance trade press does a decent job of keeping up with the basic features in regular articles — you might start with *National Underwriter*, *Rough Notes*, *The Independent Agent*, and *American Agent & Broker*. We also recommend you get the appropriate back issues, along with a subscription, to *TAAR - The Automated Agency Report* from the Automation Management Group, Inc. of Boulder, CO. With your basic reading behind you, visit other shops that have the systems in place you are considering. Talk to the front-line users there. Get competitive proposals from your one or two "finalist" vendors, and make them prove their worth.

We have seen a consensus in recent years arising from agency automation specialists that insurance retailers should budget from 3% to 5% of revenues annually for automation costs. Get used to it. Spend your money, but spend it wisely, and you won't fall behind.

Appendix 2

Letters, Mailers and Stuffers

Service or Contact Request Card

Enclose these with mailings, invoices, newsletters, etc. to keep at the front of your customer's mind when a "life change event" comes along:

Please contact me/us about the any of the following:
( ) Changing or updating some of my/our P&C coverages
( ) Adding a rider (example - purchased new home computer)
( ) Question about my/our current coverage
( ) Life insurance to pay off debts or mortgage in event of my/our death
( ) Help with changes needed to existing life insurance coverage
( ) Changed jobs/companies
( ) Change in marital status or birth of child
( ) Personalized term insurance comparison spreadsheet
( ) Other (please specify)________________________________

Name____
Phone no. ___________(ofc) _____________(home)
Best time________ am/pm
Feel free to fax this card to us at (XXX) XXX-XXXX

Mortgage Insurance Letter

Here's the body of a letter which can be used as an occasional mailer on the mortgage insurance need. Make sure that any marketing letter of this nature complies with any applicable state advertising regulations and that you only use it with approval from the company whose term cost figures you use. They know all the regulations and special footnoting required if any.

Most people feel it's important to carry mortgage life insurance to pay off the house in the event of the untimely death of one or both of the primary bread-winners. Studies have long shown that a widow's number one request in the event of a husband's death is a "paid-for" home.

Today, level term insurance rates have dropped so low that purchasing a 20- year level Term Life policy provides a very economical way to cover this risk. Premiums are guaranteed level for the entire period as is the face amount of the policy.

While you may not stay in your current home for twenty years, this term policy is entirely separate from your mortgage and mortgage company, so it is "portable" and may be used with any new mortgage on any new residence you might purchase in the future.

Here are some representative rates from one of the competitive carriers we represent for life insurance business. These are annual premiums which provide $150,000 of level death benefit coverage under a 20-year level term policy.

Age 25	$_______	Age 45	$_________
30	$_______	50	$_________
35	$_______	55	$_________
40	$_______	60	$_________

Note: These numbers assume "preferred non-tobacco" user rates and are intended for illustration purposes only. A fully-compliant National Association of Insurance Commissioner's illustration will be provided to you assuming you would like to see specific numbers for your situation.

A "Service or Contact Request Card" is enclosed for your use. Thank you again for letting us serve ALL your insurance needs.

One Extra Monthly Mortgage Payment Approach

There will be a number of other simple life product solutions which can be sold by P&C agencies who elect to just dabble in life sales. One of those which ties in nicely with the above mortgage insurance need is the "make one extra mortgage payment a year" approach to pay your mortgage off early. This can be a bit complicated to try to communicate through the mail or over the phone, but if you are meeting with the client in person, it becomes a good alternative to show in addition to the "term only" approach.

You may have heard the story about how you can pay off your mortgage years early by just making one (1) extra month's mortgage payment each year (13 payments instead of 12).

This idea sounds great in theory, but in reality somehow people get to that point when the 13th payment is due and just don't seem to ever have the extra money to make the one additional payment.

Most people feel it's important to carry mortgage life insurance to pay off the house in the event of the untimely death of one or both of the primary bread-winners! Studies have long shown that a widow's number one request in the event of a husband's death is a "paid-for" home.

By putting an amount of money about equal to one month's mortgage payment into a flexible premium universal life insurance policy, you will build up money to pay the mortgage off early.

You'd of course have run this illustration before your client comes in. All you need is their monthly mortgage payment amount. Add that to the annual term premium for either a 15-year or 20-year level term policy for the amount of their mortgage payoff. Then multiply this figure by about 1.08 or 1.09 to compensate for the monthly bank draft factor and divide this total annual figure by 12. Then run a universal life illustration using this "stated premium" and making sure you run it with a monthly premium mode. You'll be pleasantly surprised to see how much cash value accumulates in 10, 15 or 20 years which of course can either be applied against the mortgage or just used for other purposes.

Here's an example.

A 40-year old male purchases a $200,000 house and pays 20% down ($40,000) and finances $160,000 with a 30-year 8% mortgage. His monthly payment is $1,174 (principal and interest).

Running a 20-year level term proposal from any number of good carriers, the premium comes out around $400 per year, maybe less.

Therefore if you illustrate a $160,000 universal life policy and take the $400 term premium and add it to one month's mortgage payment of $1,174, you get $1,574 and if you multiply that by 1.09 to offset the bank draft factor and divide that by 12, you get around $143 per month.

That's the figure you or someone in your office plugs into the UL illustration as the "Monthly Stated Premium" figure. This figure, of course, assumes a preferred non-tobacco rate (these rates will vary greatly if you're dealing with a smoker). This approach still works fine with a smoker; you'll just have to put more money into the policy. It still should be enough to pay off the mortgage about 5 to 7 years early.

You've made a much larger premium sale and the client has cash values in lieu of only term insurance with nothing to show. Also, he or she comes to view this life insurance policy as his or her "mortgage pre-payment policy" — covering the mortgage while building values to pay it off early, meaning it should have very good persistency.

If your people were simply to concentrate on "mortgage payoff" and "basic breadwinner survivor income replacement" needs (5 to 7 times annual income is the rule of thumb), and stick with term insurance, some basic universal life or traditional whole life products, and then do regular mailings of various "checklist" cards, we will can promise results far in excess of what you are currently doing.

Appendix 3

"THE TOP 10 REASONS" Why People Procrastinate About Estate Planning

"But in this world nothing can be said to be certain, except death and taxes" -Benjamin Franklin

The following are the top ten reasons people give to put off their estate planning. Each is followed by a statement or statements that could be used to counter that reasoning when cross-selling the client such services.

Reason 10

"We need the money more than they do"

They're convinced that estate planning is really just the way that attorneys, financial planners, and life insurance agents make their living and forget that the real purpose is for their own peace of mind and their family's protection.

The cost of "doing the planning" is very low in comparison to the cost of doing nothing — Just ask Joe Robbie's family who had to sell the Miami Dolphins in order to pay federal estate taxes

Since most people associate estate planning with legal documents and "legalese," they view these documents with at least a little trepidation and are uncomfortable with them. Good estate planning attorneys will take the time to review the technical jargon with the clients and accompany the actual legal documents with a clear cover letter explaining just what's being done and why.

Insurance isn't always the best solution — the planning should be done before insurance is automatically recommended as the best or only solution

With estate taxes effectively beginning at 37 1/2% and going up as high as 60%, it is your family that stands the most to lose from not planning.

Reason 9

"I can get it done cheaper"

Because people "shop around" for almost everything these days, they sometimes believe there's going to be a less expensive way to get their estate planning done and they keep looking for it

The "Do-it-yourself" will — The person who serves as his or her own attorney has a fool for a client.

Do you really think one form can adequately deal with all issues, or the differences in each state's laws (for example in Georgia, the birth or adoption of a child revokes your will)? Also most states require that a will be signed in accordance with certain formalities - the absence of which can make the document unenforceable.

Also, you get what you pay for — In some cases, a badly drawn will can be worse than no will at all. And in even a simple estate, using an attorney who "does wills on the side" may make your family pay for his or her inexperience.

Reason 8

"It doesn't really matter. The state already has provided one for me"

Someone told them that if you died without a will, the state will take care of things because they already have a form will for you if you die "intestate" (without a will)

Do they really want the courts to be able to appoint an "administrator" for their estate and possibly a "different" person as "guardian" for any minor children?

Do you really want your 18-year old to inherit his or her share of your estate before he or she is mature enough to handle it? The BMW roadster or put it into savings and investments — which do you think would win?

A well-drafted estate plan gives your family flexibility in administering your estate — something state statutes cannot provide.

Reason 7

"I'll wait until my estate is larger"

They're sure they're either going to win the lottery or that a rich aunt or uncle is going to die and leave them millions and then they'd have to change everything in their wills and trusts anyway so why not wait. We've heard them all!

Reason 6

"Things are just too hectic today. I'll do it tomorrow."

They want to wait until things settle down: "until the office move is done;" "until we get back from vacation;" "until BIG, Inc. buys me out;" "until we see how things work out with one of our children who we're having problems with,"...but things NEVER do slow down.

Estate planning will ALWAYS be a moving target. It must be viewed as a "process" not a conclusion. It's a "snapshot" of your goals and feelings TODAY. . .remember that these will change. Why not start the process now — the conclusion could come sooner than you thought.

They're not doing the family any favors by postponing many important decisions until the decision-maker isn't around to let them know his or her true feelings. Ever have a neighbor or friend who died before life slowed down? Talk with their family how they feel.

Reason 5

"I'm not going to die any time soon. What's the rush?"

They don't want to admit the inevitable or the possible. Since they're convinced they're not going to die for another 20, 30, 40, or 50 years, why should they be concerned?

Nobody gets out of this place alive. It's not a question of whether or not you will die, it's only a question of when.

If you relate life to the four seasons of the year: Spring — birth through college; Summer — your 20s, 30s, and 40s; Fall — middle age through early retirement age; Winter — late retirement age through death, people will often have a better appreciation for how far they've already traveled through the "Seasons of Life." And sometimes they'll then even admit the journey can be cut short.

Reason 4

"I'm going to create a Living Trust"

They think they're going to put everything into a "Living Trust" to avoid all probate costs, and that's going to solve all their problems

Complex planning offers yet another excuse to procrastinate and sometimes doesn't ever get put in place whereas "simplified" planning would have sufficed. Living trusts typically involve re-titling property and transfers which sometimes never get done or aren't updated with the changing times.

The advisability of a living trust is more important in some states than others and is most appropriate when some kind of custodial situation may be in the foreseeable future due to poor health or mental incapacity.

Living "wills," medical power of attorney, and durable power of attorney are still a necessary part of an estate plan.

Reason 3

"I'm cleaning the garage out this weekend and getting my records in order"

They're waiting to get better organized. The problem is that by procrastinating, they usually put off getting everything in order and so their family will get to play "hide & seek" trying to figure out where important assets and accounts (e.g. bank accounts, important papers) are without them around.

No matter how well-intentioned, some of us will never get entirely organized. It's just not in our genes. The estate planning process forces people to begin to get organized and that usually includes writing down the location of important documents and assets.

Reason 2

"We're not rich and only rich people end up paying estate taxes"

They don't understand or appreciate how the federal estate tax works, just forget about it, or they know and try not to think about it

Some people end up leaving the government 40-60% of what they've spent a lifetime building and accumulating to spend any way it wants...instead of leaving it to their children, grandchildren, or close friends.

And even if they didn't want to leave it ALL to their children for fear of spoiling them, they still could leave the balance to the charity or cause of their choice... instead of to "Uncle Sam."

The estate tax is basically a confiscatory tax, but is *in essence* voluntary, since with proper planning you can often reduce or eliminate paying it.

Reason 1

"Who has the time? Where does the time go?

They're just too caught up in the demands of everyday living: business, kids, clubs, charity work, sports, hobbies, and even now...the Internet

The "shoe cobbler's story" — they're so busy taking care of business and other people's business, they never get around to getting their own affairs in order.

Isn't it ironic that we'll work 70-80 hour weeks building a practice, business, or career, and yet not spend just a few hours every year making sure the fruits of all our hard work go where we intend them to?

How to get started, or if you've done it and simply need to update what you have?

1. Identify a good estate planning attorney/CPA as well as an insurance or financial planning professional willing to make sure the planning gets done FIRST and that insurance is only considered as ONE of the alternatives
2. Establish your Estate and Financial Planning goals and objectives
3. Set your plan into motion. . .DO SOMETHING!

Index

E

F

G

H

I

J

L

Need Additional Copies?

Use this handy postage-paid form to order additional copies of
Crossing The Line: Sales Strategies for Life & Health in the P&C Agency
or call 1-800-543-0874 and ask for Operator RT or FAX this form to 1-800-874-1916.

Single copy $29.99	25 copies, ea. 25.50	250 copies, ea. 20.99
5 copies, ea 28.50	50 copies, ea. 23.99	500 copies, ea. 19.50
10 copies, ea 26.99	100 copies, ea. 22.50	1,000 copies, ea. 18.00

PAYMENT INFORMATION

*Add shipping & handling charges to all orders as indicated. If your order exceeds total amount listed in chart, call 1-800-543-0874 for shipping & handling charge. Any order of 10 or more or over $250.00 will be billed for shipping by actual weight, plus a handling fee. Unconditional 30 day guarantee.

Shipping & Handling (Additional)

Order Total	Shipping & handling
$10.00 to $19.99	$5.00
20.00 to 39.99	6.00
40.00 to 59.99	7.00
60.00 to 79.99	9.00
80.00 to 109.99	10.00
110.00 to 149.99	12.00
150.00 to 199.99	13.00
200.00 to 249.99	15.50

Any order of 10 or more items or over $250 will be billed by actual weight, plus a handling fee.

SALES TAX (Additional)

Sales tax is required for residents of the following states: CA, DC, FL, GA, IL, NJ, NY, OH, PA.

NATIONAL UNDERWRITER®

The National Underwriter Co.
Customer Service Dept #2-RT
505 Gest Street
Cincinnati, OH 45203-1716

2-RT

PLEASE SEND:

________ Copies of *Crossing The Line: Sales Strategies for Life & Health in the P&C Agency* (# 439)
@ $29.99 each (plus shipping & handling and any applicable sales tax).

❑ Check enclosed* ❑ Charge my VISA/MC/AmEx (circle one) ❑ Bill me

Card # ______________________ Exp. Date ______________

Signature ______________________________________

Name ______________________ Title ______________

Company ______________________________________

Street Address ______________________________________

City ______________________ State ________ Zip+4 ________

Business Phone (________) ______________________________

*Make check payable to The National Underwriter Company. Please include the appropriate shipping & handling charges and any applicable sales tax.

NATIONAL UNDERWRITER®

The National Underwriter Co.
Customer Service Dept #2-RT
505 Gest Street
Cincinnati, OH 45203-1716

2-RT

PLEASE SEND:

________ Copies of *Crossing The Line: Sales Strategies for Life & Health in the P&C Agency* (# 439)
@ $29.99 each (plus shipping & handling and any applicable sales tax).

❑ Check enclosed* ❑ Charge my VISA/MC/AmEx (circle one) ❑ Bill me

Card # ______________________ Exp. Date ______________

Signature ______________________________________

Name ______________________ Title ______________

Company ______________________________________

Street Address ______________________________________

City ______________________ State ________ Zip+4 ________

Business Phone (________) ______________________________

*Make check payable to The National Underwriter Company. Please include the appropriate shipping & handling charges and any applicable sales tax.

NO POSTAGE
NECESSARY
IF MAILED
IN THE
UNITED STATES

BUSINESS REPLY MAIL

FIRST CLASS MAIL PERMIT NO. 68 CINCINNATI, OH

POSTAGE WILL BE PAID BY ADDRESSEE

The National Underwriter Co.
Customer Service Dept. #2-RT
505 Gest Street
Cincinnati, OH 45203-9928

NO POSTAGE
NECESSARY
IF MAILED
IN THE
UNITED STATES

BUSINESS REPLY MAIL

FIRST CLASS MAIL PERMIT NO. 68 CINCINNATI, OH

POSTAGE WILL BE PAID BY ADDRESSEE

The National Underwriter Co.
Customer Service Dept. #2-RT
505 Gest Street
Cincinnati, OH 45203-9928